INVISIBLE INK:

HOW 100 GREAT AUTHORS DISAPPEARED

WITHDRAWN
FROM SUFFOLK
LIBRARIES

Christopher Fowler

Invisibl

Copyrig
Publishe

Christop
as the au
Designs :

No part
any mea P
catalogue record for this book is available from the British Library.

Suffolk County Council

30127 08330252 6	
Askews & Holts	Jun-2015
823.009	£9.99

ISBN 978-1-907222-15-3

Strange Attractor Press
BM SAP, London WC1N 3XX, UK
www.strangeattractor.co.uk

Printed in the UK

Foreword: Why Do Great Authors Disappear?

The creation of a book does not end with its publication. Often, it's where the story starts to get interesting.

Authors think when they write a novel and finally get it published, it will last forever. But most books don't, and the ones that do aren't necessarily the ones that should. The public rarely gets to choose what to save; the publishers decide which authors will be promoted and who will die of oxygen starvation. Yes, it's true that a copy will exist at the British Library, but try finding your beloved novel in a local bookshop a year after its publication; chances are you won't be able to.

This holds true in all forms of commercial art, but writers are especially vulnerable to tricks of fate, which are affected by a range of factors. Changing tastes, shrinking budgets, poor cataloguing and the need to pump the publishing spend into this month's single sure-fire title all conspire against the author. Sometimes the authors conspire against themselves. They're difficult, not pretty enough or new enough, they won't do publicity, don't interact with their readers, or simply grow sick of fruitlessly trying to sell themselves.

In the 1920s Winifred Watson was given her break not just because she'd written a good book, but because she was an attractive young secretary with great legs and a pleasing backstory, having surreptitiously written the tale in quiet moments at her office. That's not so very different from the image we hold of the young JK Rowling scribbling her Harry Potter stories on scraps of paper in a café. The fact that we remember Watson now – and will remember Rowling – is largely due to another factor: both had their books made into successful films. As long as the films stay around, the publishers are more likely to keep the original books in print. But old films find new audiences more easily than old books. You might stumble across the movie version on TV late at night and be entranced by it. It's harder to do the same on the internet with a rare paperback. The old peer groups who searched out good contemporary writing and shared it around have largely disappeared; if you want to read someone who was published fifty years ago but is out of print now, how do you know where to start?

There are always new cinema or TV interpretations of *Wuthering Heights* and *Jane Eyre*. Sherlock Holmes, Jack the Ripper and Dracula never go away, while Oz and Wonderland are painfully overfamiliar. Proliferating media platforms ensure that they're here to stay. Yet Dr Thorndyke could easily have become as popular as Sherlock, the Beetle could have beaten Dracula (and indeed did so for a while) and Mrs Bradley might have outsleuthed Miss Marple. Popular success is surprisingly arbitrary. Some authors are randomly accepted into the literary canon while others of equal talent are treasured by the discerning few. Once you make the inner temple, though – once you become a 'brand' – your novel and its characters become a critical yardstick by which to measure others. Yet even this does not future-proof you from the wilderness of lost authors. Once, readers were highly familiar with the names of Raffles, the Gentleman Crook, Bulldog Drummond, Fu Manchu, Sexton Blake and The Black Sapper, but now most casual browsers would be unable to recall their creators.

In modern times authors are expected to operate across media platforms. It's not enough to merely write; you must use a social network, run a blog, pen newspaper articles for free, appear on radio and television (if you're very lucky – writer appearances are rare now), perform before an audience, or at the very least be prepared to head off into the hinterlands to give talks in dead public spaces and appear on panels in half-empty libraries. The work is more time-consuming now than it has ever been before. Readers expect more research in their stories than they ever used to, and insist on veracity. It is no longer fashionable to write 'I arrived in the town of P---'. That town must be named, catalogued and detailed. Fiction has become harder to write, and only the physical process of writing it has become easier. The fantastical and experimental are still largely frowned upon, and copycat novels remain the safe option for publishers. At the time of writing, women's erotica is back in fashion, replacing magical schoolboys and adventures in search of religious artifacts. And shortly the wheel will turn again.

Most of an author's required ancillary activities are unwaged, or command a fee so small and irregular that only a handful reach the point where they can afford to abandon their day jobs. For many this means that writing comes after working a full day, running a family and performing the household chores. It's no wonder so many good writers simply abandon their posts.

This book began in the pages of *The Independent On*

Sunday. I'd noticed that many of my friends had never heard of the authors on my bookshelves, but fell in love with the volumes they borrowed. Writers I'd long thought of as household names had been wiped from the collective memory, and were ripe for rediscovery. These weren't esoteric narratives but popular mainstream novels from the recent past. Discussing the matter with Suzi Feay, the newspaper's terrifyingly well-read former literary editor, I realised that, unlike musicians or film-makers, authors can vanish completely. They can be ubiquitous, influential and hugely successful only to disappear, even in their own lifetimes. There are a great many authors we grew up with whose books became touchstones in our lives, who have evaporated in one or two generations. What happened to them, and why?

To find out, I began writing the 'Invisible Ink' column. I decided not to include anyone so peculiar that they had only ever attracted a specialist readership, no-one who had simply published for their own amusement or that of their friends. I was thinking of commercial fiction writers who had general appeal and proven popularity, people who had sought a living from the literary mainstream. Once their paperbacks would turn up in a chain of cheap second-hand London bookshops called the Popular Book Centres, and would be passed around at school, or end up on parents' bookshelves. Sometimes they became famous for a particular novel that touched a public nerve, but it was rarely the only thing they wrote. These authors were not One Book Wonders. Some became so popular that you would see people carrying copies of their books around everywhere you went, yet within a decade no-one could recall the titles.

The first list I compiled was from my own shelves. I'm unsentimental about books and retain very few, preferring to circulate them to friends, but I was surprised to see how many of the ones I'd kept that had lately become lost.

Publishers will always tell you two things: that there are too many books being published, and their budgets are too tight. You'd think one factor would cancel out the other. Sadly, they often have to choose between bringing out a wonderful piece of fiction that needs a little editorial work or the ghost-written kiss-and-tell biography of a very minor TV celebrity, because they know which one will guarantee sales. Recently I spent a day sitting in a bookshop in the Midlands, watching customers choose which book to buy. I think every budding popular author should do this at least once, because what you mainly see is women buying crime novels and celebrity memoirs, children buying puzzle books and men buying Jeremy Clarkson. The media and the work of PR gurus have changed our reading habits. We're time-poor and books are now more expensive, so we can't afford to be disappointed. We lessen the risk of abandoning books as much as we can.

New technology has changed this and is returning us to some unjustly neglected writers, but a surprising number are still not represented in e-libraries. Digital rights remain in a state of flux, and many of the authors represented here are not available in electronic formats. I believe that e-books will continue to sit beside hard-copy versions, partly because many books are made to be desirable objects, and their e-versions lack tactility. And it appears that the system is now also working in reverse, so that electronically rediscovered writers are proving successful enough to be republished in attractive facsimile versions.

Back in 1983, a director called Wilford Leach made a charming big budget film version of *The Pirates of Penzance*, starring Kevin Kline, Linda Ronstadt and Angela Lansbury, but nobody saw it and it vanished. Why? Because it was selected for an experimental viewing platform. The film was to premiere as the first video-on-demand item directly purchasable via the US cable network, but the public was not yet ready to accept the system, and anyway a Gilbert & Sullivan play, even one as raucously reinvented as this, was not the right film to start with. The process of creating online reading habits requires similar rethinking.

I started to ask everyone I met about their favourite neglected novelist, and it seemed everybody could name at least one. The column received startling feedback; I quickly learned that you underestimate the enthusiasm of readers at your peril. I also discovered that the modern popular paperback has an average life of six years. Cheaply printed on poor quality paper, it fades and falls apart in strong sunlight. Its publisher trashes the remainder of the print run, the author falls from popularity, stops writing, dies, or simply fails to get re-commissioned. Some publishing houses only take safe options now, and a wealth of wonderful reading is being lost. But the stories of these forgotten authors live on in our homes and our memories. They're passed to our children, to our friends, to second-hand shops. And sometimes they defy the odds and come back. Specialist imprints are currently republishing missing volumes and rediscovering lost gems.

There are other, more surprising reasons why authors disappear from bookshelves. An uncomfortable side-effect of calling any author 'forgotten' is the risk of causing offence to their family – or indeed themselves if they're still living.

Nobody wants to be thought of as vanished, but the hard truth is that shelf-life is fleeting. With the stock in chain-bookstores tracked by sales and dictated by computer, the only way of finding certain volumes is to head for independent shops or search online.

Writers were once nurtured by their publishers, who stuck with them from early success through the weaker books in the hopes of a late masterpiece, and were often rewarded. I was shocked by the number of writers who produced more than 100 books in their careers, only to completely vanish from print. After seeing the pattern repeated again and again, it started to feel like a conspiracy. Marjorie Bowen, for example, managed at least 150 volumes in her lifetime but, when I first looked, she was represented on Amazon by one anthology of short stories and a cigarette card. Readers don't forget, only bookshops (understandably so, as they have limited shelf-space and must keep their stock fresh and lively) and I relied on admirers to notify me about their favourite absent authors. It was gratifying to see that during the life of the column, some forgotten novels have started reappearing as a result of the renewed interest. The superbly odd Gladys Mitchell is back in beautiful editions courtesy of Vintage Press, while Virago, Persephone, Tartarus Press and other dedicated publishers are quietly reviving writers who've been trapped by changing tastes and times. I was particularly thrilled when New London Editions brought out *King Dido* by Alexander Baron. How did one of the best and most accessible novels ever written about London come to be lost? Sometimes the public wrongly chooses what to venerate, and publishers have their personal peccadillos. But the long memories of readers and long-tail economics may save the forgotten after all.

And thanks to new reading formats, specialised print-on-demand books have become a reality, so that some authors who vanished into obscurity have been able to bounce back and find new readers.

These are the stories, in no particular order, of the column's first one hundred forgotten authors, specially augmented for this book. A few richly deserved their fate, but a greater number should be remembered and revered by booklovers everywhere. Their work is still out there, and thanks to the work of dedicated publishers, collectors, readers and sellers, they can once more be found and enjoyed again.

1. EM Delafield

The English sense of humour is almost impossible to explain. There's a kind of amused resignation about Delafield's work. Her real name was Edmée Elizabeth Monica De La Pasture; she was the daughter of a Count, and an immensely popular and funny writer. She enlisted as a nurse in the First World War and as an Air Raid Precautions worker in the Second, and worked on a Russian collective farm. But hardly any of her thirty-plus publications can be found on bookshelves. Why did her popularity wane?

Delafield's take on life is dry and very English. Her five best books are autobiographical; *The Diary Of A Provincial Lady* chronicles her daily life as she tries to run a family and handle the housekeeping while maintaining a modicum of dignity. Written in deceptively relaxed shorthand, it's a Pooterish masterpiece of 20th century humour that shows how easily Delafield could communicate unspoken feelings of embarrassment and annoyance. Quotation is virtually impossible, as the gentle humour builds through the account of the year, but here she is at tea:

'Lady B asks me how the children are, and adds, to the table at large, that I am "A Perfect Mother". Am naturally avoided, conversationally, after this, by everybody at the teatable.' Here she is on wartime blackouts: 'Serena alleges that anonymous friend of hers goes out in the dark with extra layer of chalk-white powder so as to be seen, and resembles the Dong With The Luminous Nose. (Query: Is it in any way true that war very often brings out the best in civil population? Answer: So far as I am concerned, Not at all.)'

Perhaps Delafield's charms are not suited to coarser

times. Virago did her no favours a few years ago by shovelling four volumes of the diaries into one dense, ugly paperback prefaced with a foreword explaining why we should not find the books funny. In America, facsimiles were printed with the original delightful drawings, and found a new audience that was prepared to appreciate her qualities of grace, endurance and quiet optimism. *Diary Of A Provincial Lady* was eventually serialised for radio in the UK, but Delafield's other novels have remained virtually lost for years. The diaries are comedies of manners, but she also tackled lesbian feelings, real-life murder, alcoholism, family cruelties, adulteries and betrayals. Delafield's reasonable voice is currently out of favour, but thankfully she survives in the nation's second-hand bookshops and specialist imprints, awaiting rediscovery.

2. Geoffrey Willans

Here's an example of an author who is not quite forgotten so much as placed on the wrong shelf. The best of his charming adult books is *My Uncle Harry*, a gruesomely accurate study of the postwar British Clubman. Harry prides himself on his club tie, his stiff white collar, his rolled umbrella and his complete lack of imagination. However, it was Willans' collaboration with rococo artist Ronald Searle that was to propel him into the blazer pocket of every British schoolboy. Nigel Molesworth, the Curse of St Custard's, rocketed to fame in four lunatic children's books, starting with *Down With Skool!* With chapters on how to avoid lessons and how to torture parents, it mainly caused outrage because of its deliberately awful spelling, and was regarded as a bad example to set before New Elizabethan children.

The second diary, *How To Be Topp*, scales the heights of the surreal. A new term begins: 'No more dolies of William the bear to cuddle and hug, no more fairy stories at nanny's knee it is all aboard the fairy bus for the dungeons'. New boy Eustace is trussed to a chair and gagged with socks. His mother rings up and is reassured. 'Eustace mater ring off very relieved cheers cheers and telephone all the other lades about it. An owl hoot and Eustace is insensible. St Custards hav begun another term.'

The roster of pupils includes the ghastly Fotheringtom-Thomas, 'skipping like a girlie' and 'uterly wet', and Grabber, 'skool captane and winer of the mrs joyful prize for rafia work'. The peculiar cadences of academic lassitude are perfectly nailed, so that a recital of 'The Burial Of Sir John Moore At Corunna' becomes a bored litany trotted out by an ADD-afflicted child: 'Notadrumwasheardnotafuneralnote shut up peason larffing as his corse as his corse what is a corse sir? gosh is it to the rampart we carried'. Willans' catchphrases like 'chiz', 'enuff said' and 'as any fule kno' have passed into adult English language, but the books were meant to be enjoyed by generations of kids rather than preserved as classics, as any fule kno.

3. Margaret Millar

In the 1950s, there was a passion for psychoanalysis in US mystery novels. It underpinned Alfred Hitchcock's best films, *Psycho* and *Vertigo*, and provided the motivation for many literary murderers.

Millar was born in Kitchener, Ontario in 1915, but moved to the US and married the crime writer Ross Macdonald. She had wanted to be a writer from her teens, and eventually produced 27 novels and many short stories. What elevated them was the rich psychology of her characters. She wrote with an unsentimental eye about the lonely, the failed, the insecure and the desperate, succinctly delineating their lives in just a few well-chosen phrases. Her novels were concise and short, very much the style back in the 1950s, but the ideas they contained were unusually complex, so that her characters took on a larger life of their own.

This is a hard trick to pull off; we're used to modern mysteries clocking in at over 400 pages with everything explained and examined, often to the detriment of the book. Millar offered you a small window to a larger world. Like Shirley Jackson, she would show you the interior life of her fragile heroines, so that you could watch and empathise as they lost their grip on reality and slipped into madness. She was brilliant at revealing mental states, and her plots often hinged on the machinations of vulnerable people. Adept at creating powerful visuals, it seems hardly surprising that she made a fan of Hitchcock and ended up working at Warner Bros. Her future fame would have been assured, but Bette Davis apparently turned down the lead role in Millar's brilliant suspenser *The Iron Gates* because she was off-screen for the last third of the book, so the film was never made.

Millar was the master of the surprise ending (exemplified in *Beast In View*), carefully laying the groundwork that would lead to an entirely appropriate and organic reveal. She used three unconventional detectives, but her real interest lay in exploring the emotional lives of women of the 1940s and 1950s. The Macdonald-Millar marriage was feisty, but the arguments often resulted in the pair's best on-page dialogue. She never collaborated with her husband, but it was said that their greatest collaboration was a mutual commitment to writing.

The books fell from fashion partly because their psychology dated (one gay character kills himself after the shame of exposure) but now they can be read as period works. *Beast In View* is finally back in print.

4. Simon Raven

Simon Raven was a cad. He had a passion for privilege, no sense of obligation, a fondness for beans on toast, and too much guilt about tipping waiters to be regarded a gentleman. Nor was he upper class – his family had made their fortune from socks. Born in 1927, he set out to live a hedonistic life, and in 1945 was expelled from Charterhouse for homosexual activities. Intelligent and charming, he had a tendency to strike 18th century attitudes, marrying 'for duty' and sending the notorious telegram to his penniless wife: 'sorry no money, suggest eat baby'.

Despite just avoiding a court martial for conduct unbecoming, he enjoyed his army years and followed their instruction to be 'brief, neat and plain' in his writing. He was employed by the publisher Anthony Blond on the condition that he left London at once, as it was getting him into debt, and set about producing chronicles of upper class life, including *The Feathers Of Death* and the eerie *Doctors Wear Scarlet*, which is now regarded as something of a classic.

A pair of novel cycles, *Alms For Oblivion* and *The First-Born Of Egypt*, eventually ran (somewhat loosely) to seventeen volumes, and take on a mystical edge, although supernatural occurrences always held a fascination for him. Raven said of his writing 'I arrange words into pleasing patterns to make money', and although he never found a huge readership, he did grow more industrious.

The public became familiar with his TV adaptations of *The Pallisers* and *Edward And Mrs Simpson*, but he also wrote dialogue for *On Her Majesty's Secret Service.* His memoir *Shadows In The Grass* was described as 'the filthiest cricket book ever written', and Prion Humour Classics recently published a selection of his non-fiction writings, which include a treatise on recognising rent boys.

A gambler, *flaneur*, cricketer, controversialist, imbiber and fine host, he revelled in pushing his restaurant bills to astonishing levels. Of gambling, he cheerfully described 'the almost sexual satisfaction which comes from an evening of steady and disastrous losses.' Passionate yet aloof, dissipated yet energetic, Raven represents the perfect paradox of a certain type of Englishness. After obeying his publisher's restraining order for 34 years he returned to London and died in an almshouse for the impoverished, regretting nothing. He wrote his own epitaph; 'He shared his bottle, and when still young and appetising, his bed.' Beware the man who boasts he was a friend.

5. Horace McCoy

One of Malcolm Gladwell's rules states that the key to success in any field is partly a matter of practicing a specific task for around 10,000 hours. This seems especially true of writers; it usually takes a great deal of experience to become a debut novelist. Horace McCoy clocked up a lot of experience before writing the book for which he is most remembered.

He followed a path that will soon become familiar to readers of this book. Born in 1897, he became a bombardier in World War One, was wounded and received the *Croix de Guerre* for heroism from the French government. He had a variety of professions – sports editor, actor, journalist and writer of pulp westerns. The Great Depression saw him picking lettuces and working as a bouncer before tackling screenwriting and crime novels. He was also a script assistant on *King Kong*.

His best novel was inspired by his days working on Santa Monica pier. *They Shoot Horses, Don't They?* is a typographically innovative drama with an astonishing opening scene in which the hero casually admits to killing the girl he loves. A heartbreaking existentialist fable about a gruelling marathon dance contest in which couples must stay on their feet for a cash prize, it's also a study of the abnormal psychology that gripped California in the Depression years. The desperate couples trudge around the dance floor, and the meaning of the title quickly becomes clear as the tale assumes the weight of Greek tragedy. Understandably, America didn't take to the book at first, but the French recognised it as a masterpiece. A one-sitting read at just 125 pages, it's a masterclass in succinct writing that could teach lessons in brevity to most current writers. 'There can only be one winner, folks', says Gig Young, the unctuous MC in Sydney Pollack's excellent film version, 'but isn't that the American way?' Jane Fonda was Oscar-nominated for her role in the movie, made fourteen years after McCoy's death.

McCoy also wrote the bleak, amoral *Kiss Tomorrow Goodbye* (filmed with James Cagney) about a career criminal who is less corrupt that the local police. Two other novels bear mention. *I Should've Stayed Home* concerns jobless movie extras in sleazy 1930s Hollywood, and *No Pockets In A Shroud* is about a reporter failing in his fight against corruption.

McCoy's books have aged well. They are finally returning to visibility, thanks to publishers like Serpent's Tail and Blackmask.

6. Boileau & Narcejac

Here's an example of two good writers making one brilliant one. Pierre Boileau was born in Paris in 1903, while Pierre Ayraud, AKA Narcejac, arrived two years later in Rochefort-Sur-Mer. They were both winners of the prestigious *Prix du Roman d'Aventures,* awarded each year to the best crime novel. They both loved locked-room mysteries, both came from seafaring families and admired the classic French adventures of Arsène Lupin and Fantomas. Boileau was the first to start writing, and when Narcejac wrote an analysis of his work, they began to correspond. Growing bored with the mechanics of traditional mysteries, they wanted to explore tension and character, so two years later they started writing together. They set out to create a new style separate from English puzzle-mysteries and American violence by building ironic situations where victims, often possible murderers themselves, were more interesting than the detectives.

Like the Coen Brothers, they developed a series of writing guidelines for their dramas, the key being that the hero should not be able to wake up from his nightmare. Hitchcock chased the rights for *Les Diaboliques,* but failed to get hold of it and made *Psycho* instead. The story of a wife and mistress who set out to murder the cruel headmaster who torments them both was turned into a brilliant film with Simone Signoret, directed by Henri-Georges Clouzot.

Hitchcock enlisted the duo to adapt his masterpiece *Vertigo* for the screen. Their stories flirted with the fantastic and the macabre, erupting full-blown into the novel and film *Les Yeux Sans Visage,* with its haunting image of a woman in a china face, and gruesome monochrome scenes of surgery.

We have a 1960s Panther paperback to thank for bringing their brilliant black comedy *Choice Cuts* to the UK. It told the story of a surgeon who uses the body parts of a guillotined gunman to provide transplants, until the murderer's limbs decide to start reassembling themselves. It was filmed as *Body Parts*.

After this the pair changed tack completely, writing the *Sans Atout* books for younger readers, about a boy detective. Narcejac continued after his writing partner's death in 1990, and died eight years later. Their collection *Forty Years Of Suspense* was never published in English. As far as I can tell only two of their seventy-six works have been translated. It's staggering to think that when so much ordinary crime writing is published in the UK today, these award-winning seminal volumes still remain beyond reach.

7. George Langelaan

Although he was born in Paris in 1908, Langelaan was British, and lived a life far stranger than almost any of his fictions. By my reckoning, he didn't get published until he was approaching fifty – so what was he doing in the intervening years? Well, he began as a newspaper writer until the start of World War Two, then found himself working for British Army Intelligence. Rescued during Dunkirk after being stranded behind enemy lines, he then worked for the Special Operations Executive, a secret unit involved in sabotage and spying. To aid the French resistance movement, he agreed to be parachuted back there in order to meet a key contact, but was worried about being recognised. His ears stuck out, so along with a new identity he was given some plastic surgery to make himself less recognisable.

After being dropped he was caught by the Nazis and condemned to death, but managed to escape from the Mauzac camp in 1942. He was awarded the *Croix De Guerre*, and wrote a memoir, *The Masks Of War*, in 1959.

But two years before this he penned another work about the power of transformation. 'The Fly' was a short story that appeared in *Playboy* magazine. The tale of a scientist whose attempts to transmit himself across distances end in disaster when his cells are mixed with those of a common housefly accidentally trapped in the machine was an instant hit with readers, and was filmed with Vincent Price. The script was adapted by James Clavell, who wrote *The Great Escape*. It spawned two sequels, a remake, another sequel and an opera composed by Howard Shore, who had scored the soundtrack for the successful David Cronenberg version. Langelaan also wrote war stories, tales in French and supernatural suspensers. Alfred Hitchcock (who pops up frequently in this book) recognised his way with a good plot and adapted him for television. But despite penning two volumes of richly detailed biography, Langelaan never again achieved the level of fame he'd received for 'The Fly'.

A tale of deception and disguise, it must have been a subject close to the writer's heart, and was perhaps more of a subconscious *roman à clef* than his memoirs. But a puzzle remains; surely, if Langelaan wrote the gruesome story before suggesting his own physical alteration, it hints at something much stranger in the writer's mind – or was it merely coincidence?

8. Clifford Mills

Once upon a time, *Where The Rainbow Ends* was a book considered ideal for every young child's bedroom. In it, one illustration showed a girl being yanked into a shadowy forest by homunculi with razor-sharp claws, her pale English arms striped with crimson scars. It was captioned 'Rosalind Is Dragged Into The Black Wood By Imps'. Even as a child, I had a bad feeling about what the author was suggesting.

The author was Clifford Mills, who wrote the piece as a Christmas entertainment with music for adults and children, and opened it at the Savoy in 1911 with Jack Hawkins and Noël Coward among the forty kids in the cast. The show was produced by Italia Conti. It was *Rainbow*'s phenomenal success that led to Conti setting up her children's acting school.

In fact, 'Clifford Mills' was a woman who had taken her husband's name to write the play, which concerns an 'ordinary' group of children led by Rosamund and naval cadet Crispin (although in my edition they live in a very grand house and own a lion cub permanently dressed in red, white and blue) who are visited by St George and travel to the titular land via a threadbare magic carpet called Faith. The directions for how to reach *Where The Rainbow Ends* are hidden in a library, and Crispin summons his best friend Blunders to help. Once they reach the far-off kingdom, the children must fight their evil aunt and uncle, and take on the Dragon King. Poor Rosamund is promptly tied to a tree and left to be eaten by hyenas. St George fights the Dragon King on a tower and all ends happily.

The play became a best-selling novel that delighted

generations of children who failed to notice its jingoistic, not to say racist, tones. Much mention is made of the St George's flag and the rightness of being an Englishman, while the magic carpet genie appears to be swarthy and Jewish. A magic potion turns out to be labelled 'EMPIRE MIXTURE: Poison To Traitors' – it kills the evil uncle and aunt, and they're eaten by the hyenas. A frontispiece shows four blue-eyed blond children staring adoringly at the red and white flag. There's also a character called Schnapps, who is 'German with Jewish blood'.

Rosamund asks protection of St George by telling him 'I am an English maiden in danger and I seek your aid.' The stage play ended with St George coming to the footlights and crying out 'Rise, Youth of England, let your voices ring, For God, for Britain, and for Britain's King', at which point everyone jumped up and sang the National Anthem.

For forty years, *Where The Rainbow Ends* was as big as *Peter Pan* – it had everything: goblins, elves, a magic carpet, a battle between good and evil, songs and a cuddly animal. Unfortunately it had something else in it: the roots of fascism.

9. Holly Roth

The photograph on Holly Roth's paperbacks shows a glamorous, attractive woman in the classic 1950s mould. Born in Chicago in 1916, she grew up in Brooklyn and London, travelling the world because of her father's business. Roth eventually came to regard herself as a New Yorker. After working as a model, she started writing for newspapers and magazines. In the fifties and sixties there was plenty of fiction work to be found in weekly periodicals. Roth began writing tightly plotted suspense novels, which were serialised in *Colliers* and *The Saturday Evening Post.*

It seems likely that Roth considered herself a pulp novelist, but her books were well written and reflect the preoccupations of the times. Her thrillers were high-concept before the term had been created, and include *The Mask Of Glass*, in which Jimmy Kennemore of the US Army's Counter-Intelligence Corps wakes up in hospital injured and disfigured, his red hair turned white. Forced to piece together the events of the night that deprived him of identity, friends and a future, he discovers an international no-man's land where human life is the most expendable commodity.

In *The Sleeper*, a long-term communist sleeper agent is arrested working for the army and sentenced to life imprisonment by a military court. There's public outcry at his treatment, so the security forces conduct a PR exercise by allowing a journalist to interview him for a series of articles. Then they realise that the spy is smuggling secrets out in the quotes he's giving the writer.

In *Button, Button* (1966) a metal button with a yacht motif is a key piece of evidence in the investigation of an airline explosion that kills a heavily insured businessman. There were twelve such novels, four written under the pseudonym KG Ballard, an oddly coincidental choice of a name considering JG Ballard was a rising star at the time, but a bigger coincidence followed. In *Operation Doctors* a woman falls from a boat and loses her memory. Roth died after falling off a yacht in the Mediterranean, and her body was never recovered.

In the fifties, female suspense writers proved very popular, and Roth was compared to Mary Stewart, Charlotte Armstrong and Margaret Miller, frequently tackling the kind of Cold War-influenced subjects that have now become a strictly male province. Her books were critically overlooked at the time, and if the plots seem far-fetched, her ability to turn up the tension is unquestionable.

10. Libby Gelman-Waxner

Collected film reviews are only fun to read if their author's personality can be glimpsed through them. Leslie Halliwell always seemed a curmudgeonly nostalgist. David Thomson has the bracing acerbity of an opinionated expert. Kim Newman has an almost autistic eye for detail, but cleverly connects his reviews to the world around them.

Libby Gelman-Waxner had none of these qualities. She was a Jewish assistant buyer in juniors' activewear described as 'America's most charming and irresponsible film critic' and admitted she knew nothing about film except what she saw at the multiplex. The idea was that as 'an average filmgoer' she would bring a new perspective to reviewing. In a very short time she became the only reason for buying Rupert Murdoch's hagiographic film magazine *Premiere.*

Her reviews were hilarious because her naivety pointed up the absurdity of most Hollywood product. '*Pretty Woman* is basically a recruiting poster for prostitution', she says. 'The salespeople on Rodeo Drive snub Julia Roberts because she's tacky. What do they do when Jackie Collins starts to browse?' On the definition of *film noir*: 'sexy and really, really boring.' On ethnic-demographic movies: 'I was brought up to believe in a rainbow coalition because my mother said if a sweater is a classic you should get it in every colour.' On Tom Cruise: 'In almost all his films he learns a skill that only boys in a high school shop class would find attractive, like being a fighter pilot in peacetime, selling Lamborghinis or playing pool. In *Cocktail* he expresses emotional torment through banana daiquiris.' On Sharon Stone: 'On her tax return where it says 'profession' she can proudly have her accountant type in "Jezebel".'

Soon, though, the pieces started sneaking in an increasingly liberal political agenda. Gelman-Waxner's family members began to write for the column, including her deafening mother Sondra, her gay friend Andrew, her dentist husband Josh, and their teen daughter Jennifer. Jokes about Clinton, Foucault and Pauline Kael appeared, and the collected pieces arrived in a book called *If You Ask Me*.

Gelman-Waxner vanished from *Premiere* and the editors resigned over studio bias in its articles. In 2007 the magazine folded, and it emerged that Gelman-Waxner did not exist. 'She' was the successful screenwriter Paul Rudnick, who wrote the novels *Social Disease* and *I'll Take It*. John Cleese once wrote a book of sketches under the pseudonym 'Muriel Volestrangler'. 'Libby' was just as funny, and can now be found doing online reviews.

11. Michael Arlen

'For King and cocktails!' cries Marley, the aristocrat whose futile life is dissected in the novel *Piracy*. The world of Mayfair between the wars can make for a stifling read; all those debs and ballrooms, the spiteful point-scoring of titled couples, the calibrated snobbery of the Empire almost on its uppers now provides us with little beyond nostalgia and *Downton Abbey*. Michael Arlen was too clever to settle for merely regurgitating the antics of the fast set, but he was fascinated by its world.

The man who gave us 'When a Nightingale sang in Berkeley Square' had been born to Armenian parents in 1895, and his real name was Dikran Kouyoumdjian. When he wisely changed it, he checked a London telephone directory to make sure the English version was unique.

If F Scott Fitzgerald was the chronicler of America's abandoned jazz era, in the UK it was Michael Arlen who catalogued the hedonism of the Lost Generation. As an outsider, he determined to become the most English of gentlemen, in his appearance and in his writing. *These Charming People* contains fifteen witty vignettes of London society, but don't expect the usual arrangement of brittle dinner party epithets. The linked tales contain murder, blackmail, lost dreams, wasted opportunities and more than one ghost, presented in Arlen's casually understated dialogue.

The best was still to come. *The Green Hat* was an instant success. Its wearer, Iris Storm, is an enigmatic party girl whose younger husband defenestrates himself on their wedding night. What secret did she impart that could have caused such violence? The usual grim pattern of interference exerted itself on this smashing success; a London play version starred Tallulah Bankhead, and a travestied Hollywood film with Garbo removed the novel's dark core, excising references to venereal disease and homosexuality. Arlen was no longer an outsider, and used some of his profits to finance *The Vortex*, the first hit play from a fellow struggling writer, Noël Coward.

Arlen was now living within the society circles he portrayed. A friend of DH Lawrence (he's the basis for a character in *Lady Chatterley's Lover*), he married a countess and tried to repeat the success of *The Green Hat*, tackling science fiction and a political novel. It wasn't what the public wanted. Worse, his foreign ancestry now turned critics against him. Coward was careful never to bite society's hand; Arlen was braver and suffered for it. Happily, Capuchin Classics have reprinted him in attractive editions.

12. Alexander Baron

It's hard for frontline war writers to show an objective sensitivity to their subject matter while fighting for their country. Alexander Baron is one of the most consistently underrated British novelists of World War Two. A left-wing author and soldier who read Jane Austen in the bomb-craters of Normandy, he was interested in the psychological aspects of war, and wrote with unusual sympathy about the lives of ordinary women as well as squaddies, portraying them as essentially decent people caught in extraordinary circumstances.

Hackney-raised Alexander Bernstein was born toward the end of one world war and served in another. In the 1930s, together with his friend Ted Willis, he became a leading light in the Labour League of Youth (then affiliated with the Communist Party), but grew disillusioned with far-left politics after talking to fighters returning from the Spanish Civil War. Serving in the British Army's Pioneer Corps, he was among the first troops to land in Sicily and on D-Day, using the experience to write his first novel *From The City, From The Plough*.

He followed this with *There's No Home*, about British soldiers waiting out a lull in the war. The third part of the now highly acclaimed trilogy was *The Human Kind*, a series of linked vignettes that act as an overview of the entire war. The books benefitted from being in the first wave of popular Pan paperbacks. *The Human Kind* was turned into a Hollywood travesty called *The Victors*, with Americans replacing British war heroes.

Although he had been convinced by Jonathan Cape to change his name to Baron, he now chose to write about the tumultuous lives of gamblers and prostitutes on the streets of the East End, and the Jewish migration to suburban 1960s North London in *The Lowlife* and its sequel *Strip Jack Naked.* His epic novel of Edwardian Jewish gangs, *King Dido,* remained a personal favourite, and so it should be, for here is a tale that outlines, with infinite care, the causal link between poverty and crime. Its final pages are utterly heartbreaking, and carry tragic resonance. It is one of the greatest and least read novels about London ever written.

This postwar work was proof that serious literature could also be popular, and the shy, courteous Baron (whose failure of nerve once prevented him from attending his own launch party) now switched to film and TV. He was a regular writer on *Play For Today*, and subsequently adapted classics like *Jane Eyre*, *Vanity Fair* and *Sense And Sensibility* for television.

His elegant style and warm sense of humanity secured a reputation that's now starting to enjoy a revival. Happily, his books are once more available from Black Spring Press after years in the wilderness.

13. Philippa Pullar

Some writers never settle on a single style because their writings echo their own caprice. These are the ones who fail to fix themselves in the public attention and eventually fade from view. A singularity of thought is far more likely to win a loyal readership. Philippa Pullar has been variously described as capricious, vivacious, riotous and tormented. Born in 1935, raised conventionally in a solid middle-class West Country family, she married a chicken farmer and came to realise that her perceived notions of rural life were overly romantic.

In the seventies a number of authors began to take up their pens against the horrors of factory farming. Pullar's belief in the sanctity of animal life informed her first and greatest book, the uncategorisable *Consuming Passions: A History Of English Food And Appetite*, published in 1971. Pullar had received a Cordon Bleu Certificate of Cookery and had been a restaurant manager, so she wrote of history of food like no other, incorporating such apparently unconnected subjects as phallic worship, cannibalism, agriculture, Roman mythology, wet nursing, prostitution, witchcraft, magic, aphrodisiacs and factory canning. Her chapters include 'Pudding, Pepys and Puritanism' and 'Culinary Erections'. Her style was scattergun and frequently hilarious, incorporating recipes, jokes, historical anecdotes and a persuasive explanation about why the English lost the art of cooking – an art still only in the early stages of revival.

She explains how mediaeval cuisine was really Roman, and how spices like 'galingale, mace, cubebs and cummin' were added after the Crusaders returned with Eastern influences. There are descriptions of dinner etiquette and the experience of table gatherings, the steaming trays of cranes and swans being served, the chamberpots being passed around, the men nodding off, the women stepping into the larder 'where the jars made a cold crack on the marble shelves as the potted meats, the confections and the pickles were taken up to admire and set down again.'

Consuming Passions is not quite a history nor a cookery book, but a treatise on the art of taste, and is unique. She followed it up with a biography of Frank Harris, which was received with frosty politeness, although it is now highly regarded. Then came *Gilded Butterflies: The Rise And Fall Of The London Season*, the autobiographical *The Shortest Journey* and a descent into various New Age lunacies a friend of mine disparagingly groups together as 'Ladyscience'. *Consuming Passions* was last republished by Penguin.

14. Harry Hodge

In the modern age of phone-tapping and the super-injunction, one wonders what Harry Hodge would have said about the right to privacy. Fascinated by criminology all his life, Hodge felt that a trial should be at least 20 years old before it could prove notable enough for public discussion.

Hodge was the managing director of William Hodge & Co, publishers and shorthand writers. He followed his forebears into the shorthand business in Scotland, and became one of the nation's leading experts.

For half a century he was a well-known figure in the Scottish courts, and published many legal works. In 1905 he launched the *Notable British Trials* series, which eventually extended to over eighty volumes. In 1941, Penguin started to repackage and sell the collected *Famous Trials*, commissioned, collated and edited by Harry and later by his son James.

As the Hodges were based in Scotland, it made sense to start this catalogue of criminality with the sensational trial of Madeleine Smith, accused in 1857 of poisoning her lover with arsenic. Although the case against her was not proven, it was largely accepted that the 21-year-old beauty was a murderer, but Smith's lips remained sealed to the end of her life. The case was written up by F Tennyson Jesse, and set the elegant literary tone for the cases that followed. In the same volume we have Oscar Slater, 'the right man convicted on the wrong clue', and the tragic, bizarre tale of Dr Crippen, whose crime and subsequent arrest play out like scenes from a pulp thriller.

These are reports written closer to the time of actual events, so they've yet to be overlaid with modern forensic research or ironic asides. In outlining Crippen's case, author Filson Young sides with the doctor's murdered wife, the ghastly, tone-deaf music hall singer Belle, whereas we now have some sympathy for Crippen's impossible situation. Volume 4 of *Famous Trials* was published at the end of the war, and topically included the traitorous Lord Haw Haw, William Joyce, pointing out that radio listeners found his voice more irritating than his politics. These days, we're aware that the same propaganda tactics were being used by the British government at the time.

Volume 7 is entirely dedicated to Oscar Wilde. The series was extended to cover war crimes, and John Mortimer selected the best cases for a 1984 volume. The rest are all out of print.

15. Arthur Machen

Shockingly, a recent straw poll among young authors yielded just two recognitions of Machen's name in a group of twenty. In one sense, though, he was the Dan Brown of his time, creating elaborate Gothic novels predicated on the notion that beneath our ordinary lives was an unknown world of pagan ritual, mysticism and spirituality.

Machen was born in a modest terraced house in Caerleon, Monmouthshire in 1863, and was introduced into occult circles by his wife, a rather bohemian music teacher. The first work that brought him public attention was the novella *The Great God Pan*, which tells of the seductive, sinister Helen Vaughan, who destroys young men's lives as she takes revenge for her mother, whose sanity was destroyed after coupling with the god Pan. Published in the early 1890s, the tale was denounced as degenerate. The Wilde scandal further tarnished decadent literature, and it became hard for Machen to find publishers for his subsequent works. In 1899, the death of his wife proved a devastating blow, and he took comfort in the exploration of further pagan myths by joining the Hermetic Order of the Golden Dawn, although mysticism was a popular area of research for writers of the time.

At the start of the First World War, a legend surfaced that a group of angels had protected the British army at the Battle of Mons. In fact, Machen had written a short story for the *Evening News* called 'The Bowmen', but when the story ran it was not marked as fiction, and the Angels Of Mons shifted from fantasy to reality, in the same way that the Pope started pronouncing on the so-called truth of *The Da Vinci Code*. Machen's finances were always perilous, and his connection to the Mons legend at least brought him some degree of financial solvency.

Remarrying, he began exploring the legend of the Holy Grail. His ideas surfaced in *The Secret Glory*, which suggested that the Grail had survived to the present day. His most influential work was *The Hill of Dreams*, in which a young man recalls a childhood in rural Wales filled with sensual visions from earlier times.

His disturbing stories have had a far-reaching influence on generations of postwar writers, and his belief that the British landscape retains the imprint of those who live in it has inspired writers like Iain Sinclair and Peter Ackroyd to explore London's psychogeography. The good news is that Tartarus Press (a recurring hero in these pages) republished his best work.

16. Fergus Gwynplaine MacIntyre

Don't believe anything you read about the tweedily-dressed, bushy-haired, shambling man-mountain Fergus 'Froggy' MacIntyre. This journalist, poet, artist and bon viveur burned himself to death in a cluttered, filthy Brooklyn apartment. A Rabelaisian character who reckoned he was born in Scotland and raised in Australia, he developed an English accent and was probably from New York. His three wives and two adopted children have not been found, his name was swiped from a Victor Hugo story, his age was unknown and most anecdotes about him are contradictory.

This much is true: in 1994 he wrote a well-received steampunk thriller called *The Woman Between The Worlds* for Dell, but only managed to follow it with a volume of light poetry called *MacIntyre's Improbable Bestiary*. He was intelligent but undisciplined, loved resurrecting rare words and coining new ones, wrote reasonably good SF and fantasy short stories, book reviews, articles and crime tales, but was best at creating himself.

He said he suffered from synaesthesia, a condition in which the senses become confused, but there's no reason to assume this was true either. MacIntyre's manufactured persona evoked an English clubman's background, but the kind that is found mainly in old novels. He wore white gloves, claiming everything from torture to webbed fingers, but apparently did it to cure chronic nail biting.

In the literary world, the louche book-carrying fantasist-writer is a familiar figure. He turns up at festivals and conventions with bags full of old hardbacks, and usually behaves badly enough for others to remember him, possibly fighting with a more successful author. These are the writers who love books too much, who are full of ideas and want to take the literary world by storm, but who lack the discipline and tenacity to do so. MacIntyre enjoyed starting feuds, and one ended with the female neighbour who used to carry out his endless bags of rubbish being tied to a chair, shaved and sprayed black.

Delightful eccentricity had now given way to a damaged mental state. His career followed a downward spiral and he lost his job working nights in Manhattan as a printer. There were unusual characteristics; he was a conservative, and blogged about his pending suicide, ending with the words 'Straight on till mourning', a punning allusion to *Peter Pan.* Unlike Kyril Bonfiglioli, whose pose as a *flaneur* perfectly matched his elegant prose, Froggy allowed his constructed image to eclipse his talent.

17. Arnold Ridley

Here's a sweet story. Ridley was a one-time elementary school teacher from Bath, born in 1896, who fought in World War One and longed to be on the stage, but suffered injuries at the Somme – his left arm was badly damaged, he was bayoneted in the groin and was prone to blackouts from a fractured skull. It seemed his injuries might end his dreams of a career treading the boards, but his passion for the theatre and its memorabilia remained, and he joined the Birmingham Rep in 1918, taking a wide variety of roles before retiring when the physical wounds and mental trauma began troubling him again.

One evening he was stranded at Mangotsfield railway station, and was inspired to write a play about a mysterious train that appeared at night on a branch line, only to subsequently vanish. In *The Ghost Train*, the station through which it passes is considered to be haunted, and a group of stranded passengers have to solve its riddle. The comedy-drama was a massive hit in London and was filmed as a vehicle for Arthur Askey, so annoying in this that it was a wonder the rest of the cast didn't make him vanish too. Encouraged by his success, Ridley became the prolific author of over thirty plays between the wars, including *Keepers Of Youth*, *The Flying Fool* and *The Wrecker*, which concerned a train driver who comes to believe that his engine is possessed by a malevolent sentience.

After failing to establish a new British film company, Ridley rejoined the army in time for World War Two and saw active service in France, where he suffered flashbacks and shell shock all over again. After, he adapted an Agatha Christie novel, *Peril At End House*, for the West End, and later returned to acting, appearing in *The Archers* as Doughy Hood in the 1960s.

We remember Ridley now, not for his writing successes, but for his role in *Dad's Army* as the easily confused, mild-mannered Private Godfrey. It's ironic to think that a lance corporal who fought in the two biggest wars of the 20th century should find his equilibrium playing a committed pacifist. He continued to appear in the show into his eighties – he even appeared in the stage version, which coincided with his eightieth birthday – and was awarded an OBE. He married three times and died in 1984 at age eighty eight.

18. Charlotte Armstrong

Charlotte Armstrong was born in the iron-mining territory of Vulcan, Michigan, in 1905, and worked in the classified ads department of the *New York Times* before hitting her stride as a playwright and mystery writer. She adopted a second identity, Jo Valentine, and produced some 33 novels, hardly any of which are now in print. She wrote for the TV show *Alfred Hitchcock Presents* and Hitchcock personally directed one of her stories. It's not hard to see why he chose to do so. Armstrong wrote a very specific kind of mystery, the suspense novel. Good examples are rare now, despite what publisher blurbs may promise, but I found one Armstrong in a second-hand shop that really lived up to its name.

Mischief was written in 1951, and is a novel that unfolds in 'real time', a one-sitting read that ratchets up a feverish level of tension by watching a single situation unfold. Ruth and Peter are staying overnight at a big city hotel with their daughter, nine-year-old Bunny. Peter is in town to make an after-dinner speech, but at the last minute, they are forced to find a new babysitter. The liftman seems trustworthy, and offers the services of Nell, a girl he knows, so the couple go off to dinner leaving their daughter in her hands. However, the liftman suspects something about blank-eyed Nell that her employers don't know – she burned down her family home with her parents still inside.

When Nell loses her temper and is seen risking the child's life at a window, several hotel guests attempt to voice their concerns, but a series of miscommunications and complications merely serve to raise the stakes. This kind of simple idea, produced in bravura style, was once a mainstay of popular US suspense fiction, and was often turned into teleplays in the US. Sadly, the single play series ended after advertising demographics showed that they garnered a lower loyalty factor from viewers than long-running soaps.

Mischief became a film called *Don't Bother To Knock*, and France's answer to Hitchcock, Claude Chabrol, directed two features from Armstrong's novels. *Merci Pour Le Chocolat* starred Isabelle Huppert as a poisoner with unguessable motives, while *La Rupture* had Stéphane Audran as the victim in a murderous family drama.

Armstrong understood the motivation of her damaged characters, and drew suspense by crossing their paths with innocents. Her writing style exerts the same kind of grip Ira Levin always managed so effortlessly, and she deserves to be republished. She died in 1969.

19. Muriel Gray

Fondly remembered as a TV presenter, this cropped-blonde Scot was a tough-talking broadcaster and journalist in a time of fluffy eighties 'yoof' programming, and later appeared on our screens marching up mountains, enthusing about fell-walking. What viewers rarely suspected was that Muriel had a secret life as the author of several terrific (and terrifically creepy) supernatural thrillers.

Authors often jump genres during their careers. Certain types of plot fall from fashion, and writers must change if they are to survive. Gray decided to beat Stephen King at his own game just at the point when the overloaded genre was starting to wane. The Gothic cycle of the eighties had ended, and the public appetite for such epics appeared to be satiated. Moreover, Gray had decided to tackle a specific sub-genre within her chosen field: the Lovecraftian monstrosities born of alliances between man, myth and nature.

She started with *The Trickster* in 1994, a solid homage to King concerning native Canadian ritual magic. Four years later came *Furnace*, which showed more confidence and style. In this idiosyncratic fable, an MR James-like runic curse afflicts a long-distance truck driver in the titular Virginia town. Gray took her subjects seriously, researching in Canada, then travelling with truckers across America until she had the details down. For *The Ancient*, which begins in Lima and moves to a supertanker ferrying trash, she created another tale of ancient demonic power and outdid herself, spending several weeks on board such a ship garnering enough information for the plot, and Stephen King graciously gave the book an endorsement.

By the time Gray was married and starting a family she saw that supernatural thrillers were falling from grace, and stopped writing. I remember her describing the look of discomfort other mothers gave her at the school gates when they realised she was the wee woman writing gruesome novels of nameless evil. The supernatural cycle eventually returned, albeit in a watered-down teen-friendly form, and Gray wrote again. This time, however, she chose a very different subject. *The First Fifty: Munro-Bagging Without a Beard* is a very funny attempt to explain why some people walk up mountains for no special reason.

She has since published a work about Glaswegian art galleries, but clearly remains interested in the occult. With so few female writers tackling these kinds of grand mythologies, I hope she returns to the field.

20. Charles Dickens

There was once a comedy sketch from Monty Python precursor *At Last The 1948 Show* in which annoying bibliophile Marty Feldman tried to buy a copy of 'Rarnaby Budge' by Darles Chickens, but no – I'm talking about the actual Charles Dickens, author of such books as *The Haunted House*, *Mugby Junction*, *The Battle Of Life*, 'Going Into Society', 'Doctor Marigold' and 'A Message From The Sea'. Wait, haven't you heard of these?

Great writers tend to have their leading works repeatedly cherry-picked from the canon until we only remember those volumes, which become more familiar with each passing generation until we have to suffer through the forty third television version of *Jane Eyre* while, say, Brontë's *Shirley* and *Villette* are sidelined.

The same happened with the astoundingly prolific Dickens, who wrote short story collections, non-fiction, children's works, supernatural tales, sketches, dramatic monologues, Christmas fables and a dozen collaborative works. To complicate matters, some books had excerpts removed to be tailored into individual stories. Let's not even go into his poetry, plays, essays and journalism.

The charming *A Child's History Of England* is so chatty and informal that it probably provided a blueprint for today's hugely successful *Horrible Histories* series. His chapter on Henry VIII begins 'We now come to King Henry The Eighth, whom it has been too much the fashion to call Bluff King Hall or Burly King Henry and other fine names, but whom I shall take the liberty to call, plainly, one of the most detestable villains that ever drew breath.' No mincing words there.

Mugby Junction is a collaboration compiled by Dickens in which stories ranging from the eerie to the comic are interwoven around a bustling train station. When the narrator sees a deserted house from his railway carriage in *The Haunted House*, he ignores local legends and takes up residence with a group of friends. The resulting multi-part Dickensian novel has contributions from Elizabeth Gaskell and Wilkie Collins among others. Dickens often wrote with Collins, but does that make his stories 'impure' and therefore less canonical? It seems odd that we should face annual remakes of *A Christmas Carol* while *A Christmas Tree* and the *Mrs Lirriper* Christmas stories are overlooked.

Not all of the neglected shorter prose is perfect, but it seems well-suited for downloading as e-reading, and is absurdly cheap. Dickens' less visible works are not out of print but have been collected too often in different formats, so that tracking them down without duplication was pretty tricky work until electronic formats arrived.

21. Caryl Brahms and SJ Simon

How did the English cheer themselves up during wartime? One of the ways was by turning to the sprightly comic novels of this unlikely duo.

She was born into a Sephardic Jewish family in Croydon, he was born in Manchuria. She trained as a musician and wrote ballet criticism, he was a genius bridge player, winning tournaments, writing books on card systems and becoming the bridge correspondent of *The Observer*, when there were such things. Caryl (née Doris Abrahams) Brahms and 'Skid' (ne Simon Skidelsky) met in a hostel and shared the same ridiculous sense of humour. First they wrote captions for David Low's political cartoons in the *Evening Standard*, then they graduated to crime novels.

A Bullet In The Ballet (1937) was the result of a delayed meeting and a conversation over a cup of tea. Brahms did the ballet bits, and Skid wrote the parts that involved detection. A dancer is shot in the head during a production of *Petrushka*, and Detective Inspector Quill, 'the Scotland Yard Adonis', is dispatched to uncover the killer, only to find that the *corps de ballet* is filled with vipers. The novel's first line is 'Since it is probable that any book flying a bullet in its title is going to produce a corpse sooner or later – here it is.' It was followed by a ballet-themed sequel, *Casino For Sale*, the following year. Both feature the high-living impresario Vladimir Stroganoff, a hilarious creation who deserved his own series. Curiously, my edition of *A Bullet In The Ballet* suggests that I might also enjoy reading *A Survey Of Russian Music*, which may be an indication of the thoroughness of Brahms' research.

Envoy On Excursion is a European farce with Nazis,

somewhat akin to *The Lady Vanishes*, and *Six Curtains For Stroganova* concludes the set with the same characters. Farce should never outstay its welcome, and all the books are short but packed with merriment. The duo also wrote excellent historical farces, the best being *No Bed For Bacon*, which was very obviously the unacknowledged inspiration for *Shakespeare In Love*, and *Don't, Mr Disraeli*, which includes virtually every clean Victorian joke you can think of, plus a cameo from the Marx Brothers. There are other volumes, and assorted short stories featuring the Brahms and Simon characters, but these are out of print. Somebody, please republish! After Simon's death, Brahms continued writing and adapting farces with Ned Sherrin.

22. Sarah Caudwell

Sarah Cockburn was the pipe-smoking daughter of the left-wing journalist Claude Cockburn. Her step-mother was partly the model for Christopher Isherwood's Sally Bowles and her family was full of journalists, so it's hardly surprising that she grew up with a strong-willed nature. She was one of the first female students to speak in the Oxford Union's Debating Chamber, having apparently dressed in male clothes to protest the Union's male-only policy, thereafter gaining membership.

She became a barrister and under the name Caudwell, adopted to provide some distance from her profession, wrote a series of legal thrillers set on the top floor of 62, New Square in Lincoln's Inn, where four barristers have their chambers. Presiding over them is the narrator and professor of medieval law, Hilary Tamar, the only detective I can think of whose sex is never determined. Tamar uses the barristers as a kind of ironic, adult Enid Blyton gang to help her solve crimes, and they in turn keep her in touch with what's going on by posting absurdly long letters and sending telexes.

The first in the series was *Thus Was Adonis Murdered*, published in 1981. Three more volumes followed. Caudwell used her knowledge of tax and inheritance laws to add realism to the cases, but apart from that they're quite potty, with members of the team tromping around exotic locations dropping barbed *bons mots* to their mentor. The tone is exhaustingly literary, witty and dry, and the stories are deliberately constructed as Golden Age confections, in an extension of the style that Edmund Crispin and Michael Innes had established before her. *The Shortest Way To Hades* has a family tree and a thirties-style room plan showing the crime scene. Her lifelong love of crossword puzzles is evident in her fascination with word-play.

Caudwell's books have maintained their appeal and stature, and she is now being reassessed as A Good Thing. She also wrote a number of short stories and comic pieces, and contributed to an enjoyable multi-author work called *Perfect Murder: Five Great Mystery Writers Create The Perfect Crime*. There was one play, a drama about the case to establish the legal standard for defining sanity in law, but I'm not aware that it was performed. She was a painfully slow writer, and her publishers grew tired of waiting for another book from her. Sadly, she died of cancer before its final publication.

23. Gavin Lambert

After a Hollywood orgy, a beautiful young girl emerges from a swimming pool in morning light. 'Is there anyone you should call?' asks the host, 'anyone who'll be wondering where you are?' 'No, there's no-one in the world', she replies.

Meanwhile, as he realises he is losing the one commodity that makes others love him, an ageing star's easy charisma dies in the panic for survival. 'When time's running out', he notes, 'you get a touch of the fever.'

Welcome to the world of Gavin Lambert, a gay British scribe in Hollywood and a close friend of Natalie Wood and Paul Bowles. For this author of seven novels and half a dozen screen biographies, Hollywood's paradox never changed: how could so many men and women attempt to prove their individuality in a place that actively discourages independent thinking? It's an idea that raises the dramatic stakes between success and failure.

Lambert tracked these aimless lives across decades in a *Hollywood Quartet* of novels. The best-known, *Inside Daisy Clover*, was written (and filmed with Natalie Wood) in the sixties, and *The Goodbye People* appeared at the start of the seventies, by which time the dream had truly soured, and the unscrupulous behaviour of studio bosses paled into insignificance beside the waking nightmares of Manson and Nixon.

The Goodbye People is not an industry novel; its characters only brush against the film world, but their lives are affected by the dreamlike hedonism that wafts temptingly around them. The people of Southern California are presented as separate tribes that only cross paths when their chieftains visit each other during festivals, and the world outside is something you see from a car. Lambert's characters are badly behaved children, narcissistic, selfish and manipulative. They're forever changing their addresses and phone numbers, but can't decide who they're running from.

His writing is wry, spare and non-judgmental, which keeps his style modern. Lambert was in a position to know his world. He wrote the screenplays for *Sons And Lovers* and *The Roman Spring Of Mrs. Stone*, and was twice nominated for Academy Awards. *The Goodbye People* is his dark glory, melancholic, becalmed and effortlessly resonant. Its greatest strength is its delineation of a town that disfigures all with its luxurious blankness. Only his 1959 classic *The Slide Area* (named after the land along Pacific Palisades that is 'likely to slip away without warning') remained in print; the rest slipped away much like his lonely, disillusioned characters. Nothing much happens in Lambert's books – he was less concerned with plotting, which is generally as arbitrary as the weekend plans of his cast, and more interested in pinning on the page characters who possess powers of attraction 'like gravity, natural and immediate.' What disturbs most is the thought that his studies of lost lives are just as accurate today as they were when he wrote them. In *The Goodbye People*, the hero explains that he doesn't read books because the characters always get somewhere, and this frustrates him. 'Isn't that the trouble with most books?' he asks. 'They look so good on paper.'

24. One-Hit Wonders

Beware the book that bears the legend 'Soon To Be A Major Film', for the film won't be made and the book is bound to vanish. Such was the fate of *The Auctioneer* by Joan Samson, a novel that took America by storm and became a bestseller. Hollywood came calling, and then – nothing. Samson only completed this one novel in her lifetime, although she was working on a second at the time of her death. *The Auctioneer* uses a popular trope in US literature, the dark stranger who arrives in town and causes havoc. Perly Dunsmore is a charismatic auctioneer who arrives with a request for donations to support the police, and as his power grows the townspeople soon find themselves surrendering a lot more than their rusty tools and dusty furniture. The tale is a fable about the spiralling effect of power, and has been published in a new edition.

Charles MacLean writes one novel every decade, and his astonishing metaphysical page-turner *The Watcher* was optioned in the early 1980s by, if memory serves, none other than Paul Newman, who planned to film it. It seems likely that he never managed to crack the on-screen presentation of the first scene, in which the nice, ordinary hero Martin Gregory takes an electric carving knife to his wife's dogs. Gregory has no idea why he should commit this bizarre atrocity, and psychiatric scrutiny reveals his action to be the outward result of a much greater ongoing war involving past lives. Stephen King was influenced by the book enough to write an homage, *Needful Things.*

A happier fate befell another one-off, *Burnt Offerings* by Robert Marasco, a classic haunted house thriller in which the supernatural is used to explore the pressures of modern life. A seemingly perfect family comes apart at the seams after moving to a beautiful white clapboard house. Father attacks son, wife grows distrustful, mother ages from feistiness to senility, and as their misery compounds the house flourishes. This one made it to the screen with the unlikely acting combination of hellraisers Bette Davis and Oliver Reed.

One-hit wonders are more trouble to publishers than they're worth; create a readership for the book and the readers may have nowhere else to go. The twisting psychological thriller *Blood Secrets* by Craig Jones played like a non-supernatural *Rosemary's Baby* and was championed by John Irving. Hollywood came calling. By now you know the rest.

25. Brian Moore

There are too many Brian Moores. One is rugby's hard man, the uncompromising commentator who has several biographies. The less-discovered Moore is the Irish-Canadian novelist who wrote a number of haunting novels, often concerning life in Northern Ireland, exploring the Troubles and the Blitz. Born into a family of nine children in Belfast, 1921, he rejected Catholicism and explained his personal beliefs through the characters of torn priests and strong women.

Not that you'd know this from his early works; *Wreath For A Redhead*, *This Gun For Gloria* and *A Bullet For My Lady* aren't exactly masterpieces. Moore wrote thrillers under two pseudonyms while perfecting his craft. Then came *Judith Hearne*, the story of an alcoholic piano teacher subsisting in rented rooms which gains its heartbreaking power from the simplicity of clear prose. It was later filmed as *The Lonely Passion Of Judith Hearne* with Maggie Smith and Bob Hoskins, but the movie is now hard to find. Five of his novels became films, and he scripted for both Alfred Hitchcock and Claude Chabrol, although he described the writing of *Torn Curtain* as 'awful, like washing floors'.

Financed by a grant from the Guggenheim, Moore moved to New York. He often returned to the subject of isolated outsiders facing the consequences of their actions, from the rabble-rousing missionary in *No Other Life* and the fascist officer awaiting discovery in *The Statement* to the conflicted priest living among Canada's Algonquin Indians in the harrowing *Black Robe*.

He was Graham Greene's favourite living novelist, mainly, one suspects, because he was able to explore the paradoxical dilemmas of faith, morality, redemption and loss within the structure of popular thriller writing. In *The Magician's Wife*, a Parisian prestidigitator is dispatched to Algeria by Emperor Napoleon III to trick the natives into believing that a Christian Frenchman can perform miracles, but his wife is not so easily hoodwinked. It's a typical *tour de force* from a novelist who was thrice nominated for the Booker Prize, and the subject of three biographies.

Perhaps his least appreciated novel is *The Great Victorian Collection*, an exuberant fantasy in which a young assistant history professor dreams of an open-air market filled with a dazzling collection of priceless Victoriana, only to awake and find it standing outside his window. But, as we know, possessions come with a price. His books are effortless to read, pithy and unfashionably short. Moore died in 1999. A few of his novels are published by Paladin.

26. Maurice Richardson

Here's a forgotten author with a single remembered book to his name, but what a book! The paper shortages of the Second World War gave rise to *Lilliput Magazine*, a diminutive periodical that survived thanks to the quality of its writers and illustrators, who included Richardson, Nancy Mitford, Stephen Potter, Mervyn Peake, VS Pritchett, Ronald Searle, Robert Graves, Aleister Crowley, Patrick Campbell, Gerard Hoffnung and Sir Max Beerbohm. It helped that they published fairly saucy (for the time) pictures of unclothed ladies. Every cover featured a scene combining a man, a woman and a dog.

Maurice Richardson was born in 1907, a manic-depressive ex-amateur boxer and journalist who hung out with a pretty low-life crowd. He reviewed books throughout his life and died in 1978. A classic example of a talented man with too many interests, most of Richardson's writings and books, like *Little Victims*, *Fits And Starts* and *The Fascination Of Reptiles* have left no trace. His great success was unexpected: a compendium of linked pieces that has remained in print through the decades. *The Exploits Of Engelbrecht* was loved by JG Ballard, and is certainly one of the most unusual books ever published.

Engelbrecht is a dwarf Surrealist boxer who goes ten rounds with a grandfather clock (needless to say, his opponent gets punched in the dial) but he's an all-round sportsman who'll tackle any game, no matter how peculiar it gets. We first meet him taking part in a witch hunt that unfolds like the Glorious Twelfth, then at a golf game which takes him around the world in one course. When he battles a demon bowler, the bowler is naturally, a real demon – the innings closes at 3,333,333 for 9. The Surrealist sporting calendar is filled with alarming events like the Interplanetary Challenge Cup, where Engelbrecht and teammate Salvador Dali thrash the Martians on the Moon.

Engelbrecht may take all night to wrestle the Kraken and get involved in an angling competition that shares the nightmarish quality of a Hieronymus Bosch painting, but he is also a man of culture: he attends the Plant Theatre and the Dog's Opera (the contralto is a Great Dane and the libretto is in Dog-Latin) before eloping with a cuckoo clock.

The Exploits Of Engelbrecht is currently available in an illustrated edition from Savoy Books, who have supplemented it with Richardson's wedding report involving Holmes, Moriarty, Dracula, Frankenstein and Poirot.

27. Barbara Pym

Few careers are more easily destroyed than by a sudden fall from fashion. Some writers return to popularity, but none in such a spectacular manner as Pym, a quintessentially English novelist whose twelve miniaturist novels can now be described as both popular and timeless.

Pym was born in Oswestry, Shropshire, one year before the Great War. She attempted her first book, *Young Men In Fancy Dress* at 16 and her second, *Some Tame Gazelle* at 22, periodically submitting it to publishers who always turned it down. She wrote about characters she knew and understood. Her mother was a church organist, so vicars and curates inevitably appeared in her books. She and her sister Hilary featured in the second, projected into the future as spinsters, and anthropologists tended to crop up because of her years spent working at London's International African Institute.

By the time another world war broke out, she had still not been published. After, she and Hilary moved to a flat in Pimlico, and she wrote stories for women's magazines without any real success.

Then, in 1950, Jonathan Cape published a revised version of *Some Tame Gazelle*, finally launching her career. Pym's first six books established her as a unique voice. Her plots left faint impressions but her style allowed her to explore the lives of unassuming, genteel characters with clarity and originality. She found her voice and her audience.

In 1963, disaster struck. *An Unsuitable Attachment* was returned without a contract; in the era of the Beatles, she had fallen out of step with the times. Shattered by the rejection, she felt that no-one would ever admire her style of writing again. Further books were rejected as publishers swept out their cupboards and chased new trends.

On January 21st 1977, after sixteen years of obscurity, Pym was named 'the most underrated novelist of the 20th century' by both Lord David Cecil and Philip Larkin in *The Times Literary Supplement.* Overnight, her books were published (but not by Cape), she was shortlisted for the Booker Prize and discovered a huge, eager new audience in America.

Only two years after her rediscovery, she succumbed to a recurrence of breast cancer. She said 'The small things of life were often so much bigger than the great things. The trivial pleasures like cooking, one's home, little poems especially sad ones, solitary walks, funny things seen and overheard.' She is buried beside her beloved sister.

28. Robert Louis Stevenson

Yes, we know you had a tattered copy of *Treasure Island* in your schoolbag when you were ten (worth rereading for its unique structure, in which all of the main events have occurred before the book's start), you're aware of *Kidnapped* and *The Strange Case of Dr Jekyll and Mr Hyde*, but did you know that the best part of his career is now the least remembered?

The range and complexity of Stevenson's short fiction is extraordinary. Although he is known for the graceful construction of his plots, he was a champion of literary style throughout his life, and feared it was dying out in his own country. As a child, one of Stevenson's favourite books had been the original *Arabian Nights*, so he wrote the *New Arabian Nights*, which featured two interlinking sets of tales, *The Suicide Club* and *The Rajah's Diamond*. In these stories, the dashing Prince Florizel and his sidekick Colonel Geraldine leave their Rupert Street abode and hop into hansoms, setting off on nocturnal adventures involving secret societies and sinister plots to overthrow order.

You can trace this macabre strand of Stevenson's writing to his reckless student life in Edinburgh, which brings us to the Conan Doyle conjunction – why is Sherlock Holmes so ubiquitous while Stevenson's hero is forgotten? Well, there's a matter of quantity. After all, we have 56 Sherlock short stories and four novels from Conan Doyle. But we even tend to recall Stevenson's better-known tales wrongly. Mr Hyde, for example, is no physical monster but has the spiritual malignance of Dorian Gray, and the antidote he needs lies in the warmth of human relationships.

Stevenson cherished lasting friendships and found in

them the solution to most human malaises. The characters in his darker tales, like those in 'Markheim' and 'Thrawn Janet', are lonely and loveless. His later exotic fables were inspired by his own travels in the South Seas, and 'The Bottle Imp' is the best genie-in-a-bottle story ever, partly because of the dilemma it imposes upon any owner, for the bottle must always be sold on for less than was paid for it.

Stevenson's stories may have been overlooked by modern readers, but not by other authors. His influence can be seen in the works of Kipling, Hemingway, Nabokov, JM Barrie, Arthur Machen and GK Chesterton. He was a literary superstar in his short lifetime, but it didn't guarantee immortality for much of his best work. Happily, Tartarus Press reissued *The Suicide Club & Other Dark Adventures* in a handsome hardback.

29. Peter Nichols

While novels remain yellowing on shelves, most plays are entirely ephemeral, vanishing after a brief trot around the theatre circuit. Nichols' plays proved more robust and cinematic – several were filmed – but that hasn't stopped him from disappearing in a West End glutted with musicals.

Nichols was born in Bristol in 1927, which threw him into the war in his teens. A contemporary of the equally brilliant Charles Wood, he began writing television plays (when there were such things) but where Wood frequently wrote about war and survival, Nichols has always been harder to pin down in choice of subject matter. His work was often autobiographical. *A Day In The Death Of Joe Egg* had been inspired by his own experiences of raising a handicapped child, and although a deeply compassionate piece, it's still profoundly shocking today.

He clearly enjoyed making audiences uncomfortable. *The National Health* was a zeitgeist play presenting Britain as an ailing patient, as soap-opera medics fall in love while, in the real world, an imploding NHS hospital proves unable to cope with the sick, who die in an atmosphere of indifference. *Privates On Parade* rendered Nichols' ENSA experiences into dramatic form as the ditzy members of the Song And Dance Unit South East Asia, under the command of queeny Captain Terri Dennis, end up running guns on a hellish tour of Malaysia that sees most of them shot dead or wounded. Dennis is a glorious creation, camp and brave, with a penchant for the dressing up box and a disrespectful range of one-liners: 'That Bernadette Shaw, nags away from arsehole to breakfast-time but never sees what's staring her in the face.'

Nichols' most subversive play was *Poppy!* which reimagined the Chinese opium wars in the form of a Christmas pantomime complete with panto cow, dame and cross-dressed principle boy. At one point the audience was encouraged to rise and join in a singalong about the disgraceful behaviour of British troops, while Dick Whittington's sister ends up a junkie. That this could be installed at the Adelphi Theatre in a spectacular RSC production says a lot about theatreland's present low ambitions. A terrific autobiography, *Feeling You're Behind*, followed, along with an excellent set of diaries covering Nichols' key years. Clearly, the West End needs his angry humanity more than ever.

30. Frank Baker

Who wrote the story on which Alfred Hitchcock based his film *The Birds*? Before you say Daphne Du Maurier, read this. Thirty years before Du Maurier's short story, Frank Baker wrote *The Birds*, in which London's inhabitants were turned upon by avian predators. Although Baker's version was much more ambitious, the stories are remarkably similar, and like Du Maurier, Baker was also living in Cornwall. Was it coincidence or something more? Baker's birds seemed more supernatural in origin, but he was naturally upset and corresponded with Du Maurier, who sympathised. Hitchcock, who seems to have followed Baker's version more, ignored the likeable young church organist, who was somehow persuaded not to pursue costly litigation against Universal Studios.

Baker was born in Hornsey, London in 1908, and moved to St Just In Penwith, where he began to write. In 1935 his first novel *The Twisted Tree* was published – an odd choice for a man who sought religious comfort (partly, one suspects, because of rumoured issues with his sexuality). It told the story of a woman who gives birth to a child who turns out to be a monster.

Although Baker was drawn to the whimsical, he grounded his novels with recognisable characters and locations. *Mr Allenby Loses His Way* (1946) reflected this curious mix of realism and fantasy. In it, a fat little shopkeeper leaves his family to discover his true magical identity. This morality tale of belief and the demands of social conformity is haunted by the war and by Baker's own self-doubts. Of his fifteen novels, his masterpiece is the enchanting *Miss Hargreaves*, in which two friends on holiday in Ireland are required to invent the titular 83-year-old woman. Later, forced to explain how they met her, they slowly add details to her life, embellishing her backstory with the information that she always travels with a cockatoo, a harp and her own bath.

The lark gets out of hand when they receive a telegram from Miss Hargreaves herself, informing them that she is coming to stay for an indefinite period – but how can they explain who she is when they can't even understand why she exists? A comedy about the creative imagination, loss of control and the pressures of conformity, *Miss Hargreaves* came to the London stage starring Margaret Rutherford, the living embodiment of the character and a friend of the author. His novel *Lease Of Life* was filmed with Robert Donat. *Miss Hargreaves* is once more available in print.

31. John Burke

How can you be forgotten if you've deliberately avoided having an identity to begin with? That's the challenge of pinning down John Burke's work.

In the past, not all authors were determined to produce the great *roman à clef* that would make sense of their lives. Many were simply available for hire, and would turn their hand to just about anything. This was not an easy way to make a living, because the writer's prose was not allowed to possess its own identity. Jobbing authors were required to submerge their stylistic quirks in the service of the product.

Occasionally, though, an author would come along who managed to combine both skills. Sussex-born John Burke, born 1922, has worked under at least ten names, also writing Victorian Gothic romances with his wife Jean beneath the pseudonym Harriet Esmond. He mainly specialised in what has become something of a lost art: the novelisation of the film. His paperbacks for Hammer have stunning covers and each contain four condensed movie novelisations. They are now highly collectable. His backlist reads like a summation of postwar pop culture. He wrote versions of *Look Back In Anger* (which must have been odd for John Osborne), *Chitty Chitty Bang Bang* (likewise for Roald Dahl), *The Entertainer*, *The Angry Silence*, *The Jokers*, *A Hard Day's Night*, *Privilege* and *Dr Terror's House Of Horrors*, before turning to TV spinoffs like *Dad's Army* and books about *The Bill*. Often, his narratives feel more structurally cohesive than the works upon which they were based, and have a clearly identifiable style that marks them with the author's imprimatur.

But Burke has another identity, as the Master of Unease.

A superb short story writer, some of his best and most chilling works were recently collected in a single volume by Ash Tree Press, entitled *We've Been Waiting For You (And Other Tales Of Unease)*. He has produced books on the history of England, its counties and its music, science fiction novels and thrillers, and television series. Happily, he's still working and has just finished a sequence of mystery novels set in the Scottish borders.

It seems the time has come for Burke to step out from behind his books and receive proper recognition for his work. Ironically, an author once employed for his ability to be the film industry's chameleon is finally being rediscovered as a prose stylist in his own right.

32. Rosalind Erskine

Sometimes I stumble across a strange old paperback, investigate the author and discover something even more tantalising. In 1962, Erskine's novel *The Passion Flower Hotel* caused a sensation and became a bestseller. It tells the story of Bryant House, an exclusive private girls' school, where the sixth-formers find themselves unable to meet boys and learn about sex. Over at Longcombe school for boys, the same problem exists. The solution is still shocking: the girls set up a brothel in the school basement, with a menu of categories and prices.

At the time of the book's publication it was virtually impossible for pupils in private schooling to mix sexes, unless you counted events like the annual opera, where schools teamed up to provide the right gender balance. The original St Trinian's films had already tackled the tricky subject of schoolgirl sexuality, and the Passion Flowers of Bryant House riotously smashed down the walls. The book spawned two inferior sequels, a terrible German-made film and even a hit West End musical with a lush Bond-like score written by John Barry.

The big selling point was its author, 15 year-old Rosalind Erskine, supposedly being educated at just such a school. Misinformation abounded about her – did she even exist?

The answer is of course not. Rosalind was Roger Erskine Longrigg, the creative director of an advertising agency, who had recognised that the time had come for a smartly written erotic comic novel. The book is a joyful and oddly innocent romp, but would probably have risked opprobrium had it been published under a male identity.

Longrigg was a Scot from a military background who

published two books about his experiences in the ad game, *A High Pitched Buzz* and *Switchboard*. Recently unearthed by Faber, they now feel like the British answer to *Mad Men*. Longrigg went on to write 55 novels under eight different names, choosing a male or female persona appropriate to each work. His prose is sparkling and epithetical, and his career stayed buoyant for decades. He was married to the novelist Jane Chichester.

Later, writing as Domini Taylor, Longrigg produced the 1983 novel *Mother Love*, which was filmed for television with Diana Rigg and David McCallum. He also wrote about fox hunting and horse racing, and proved pretty successful at any subject he turned to. But he'll be best remembered for the saucy Passion Flowers, even though the book is sadly now out of print.

33. Stacy Aumonier

There's something Christmassy about Stacy Aumonier. His *Extremely Entertaining Short Stories* feel as if they should be read aloud by a roaring fire. He was born near Regent's Park into a family of craftsmen and artists in 1877, and reached 51 before dying of tuberculosis. During this time he wrote many short stories which should rightly be regarded as classics – but it didn't happen. Worse, his work has vanished completely, and even collections of tales get his dates wrong. Yet John Galsworthy and Alfred Hitchcock were admirers of his page-turning style, his way with suspense, his wit, humanity and lightness of touch. He was described as 'never heavy, never boring, never really trivial.'

The more I heard about Aumonier, the more I began to suspect I was the subject of a hoax. Did he really come from an entire family of sculptors? What was his Tutankhamun connection? Could he actually have married a concert pianist called Gertrude Peppercorn? He certainly wrote a novel about a wartime family, *The Querrils*, and a book called *Odd Fish*, about the eccentric residents of a London street. He sat for rather a lot of paintings in the National Portrait Gallery, which usually show him dressed for dinner. He wrote enough suspense to draw the attention of Hitchcock, who filmed television versions of some of his stories. Beyond this, the trail disappears.

And yet his reputation doggedly persists. Phaeton, who most recently revived his tales, say 'the more we probed into his background, the more we liked him.' In the 1920s, he became unrivalled as a short story writer. In one of his most famous tales, 'Miss Bracegirdle Does Her Duty', the shy, untraveled heroine winds up underneath a dead stranger's bed in a French hotel room. In 'A Source Of Irritation', an elderly farmer is kidnapped by an enemy pilot who crashes in his field. In 'Where Was Wych Street?' an argument in a pub escalates into a full-blown siege. He wrote about idiosyncratic people being pushed to conform and bucking their fate, and like O Henry and Saki, was capable of condensing a life into a few pages. When he was fatally diagnosed, he wrote 'The Thrill Of Being Ill', in which he says 'You become subtly aware of the change in attitude in the manner of certain people… you have become dramatically a centre of interest.' It takes a certain courage to continue finding pleasures at such a time.

34. Virginia Andrews

Sometimes an author's work lives on, but here's an example of an actual author living beyond her death. Or rather, not – because the real Virginia Andrews has been forgotten and replaced by a ghost writer called Andrew Neiderman, who has penned over forty subsequent volumes in her name. Andrews' books did so well that her estate found it necessary to keep her alive and continue earning money. The Inland Revenue Service even argued that her name was a valuable, and therefore taxable, asset.

In the age of the brand, this publishing behaviour is becoming more and more the norm. We've had extensions of everything from Sherlock Holmes to *Sense And Sensibility*, because they come with a built-in readership. But let's go back to the beginning of the Andrews story.

Cleo Virginia Andrews was an American novelist born in 1923, in Virginia. She started out as an illustrator and portrait painter, a sedentary occupation chosen largely because she was crippled by arthritis stemming from problems compounded by an early fall. When she switched to writing at the relatively late age of 55, she first chose science fiction, then produced a novel called *The Obsessed*, which her publisher felt she should sex up and retitle. The revised version, a perverse fairytale marketed as a horror novel and now called *Flowers In The Attic*, appeared in 1979 and became a surprise bestseller. It's an airless, claustrophobic work, telling the story of four blonde blue-eyed siblings, Cathy, Cory, Carrie and Chris, who are imprisoned in an attic by their mother and grandmother in order to gain an inheritance. Kept there for years, mentally and physically abused by their relatives, two of the children eventually fall in love and form a new family unit before escaping.

The siblings wreak revenge on their captors in the second novel, and subsequent sequels continue the style from new viewpoints. Throughout, Gothic imagery is laced with all the trappings of Victorian melodramas; there are hidden identities, arsenic poisonings and outbreaks of religious hysteria, complete with outbreaks of arson, incest and incarceration in madhouses. It seems that the feverish hothouse atmosphere of life in the attic appealed to the temperament of teenaged girls, who clearly wanted to have their most macabre fears about sex confirmed, and bought the books in their millions.

Andrews' stand-alone novel *My Sweet Audrina* explored similar themes in outlandishly lurid prose. She began another series, but soon these volumes were only 'inspired' by her voluminous notes as, by this time, Andrews had inconveniently died. The original books are psychologically unsettling and compellingly awful, whereas the pseudonymous volumes which were designed to keep the brand alive are merely awful.

35. Thomas Love Peacock

To say that Peacock is an acquired taste is something of an understatement. The English satirist was born 1785 in a naval family. He moved to London in his teens, became a city clerk and taught himself poetry at the British Museum's Reading Room. Earning his crust as a private secretary to a naval fleet commander, he began to make a serious study of French, Italian and English literature. His minor poems (including one long one about the Thames, which he loved all his life) brought him to the attention of Shelley, who recognised his virtues as a romantic classicist. They remained close friends until the latter's death in 1822. Peacock wrote a series of seven satirical novels which remain impossible to categorise and challenging to read.

For a satirist Peacock is remarkably good-natured, but his novels are rambling, vague and highly peculiar – so why should we remember him? Probably because there really is no-one else quite like him; *Nightmare Abbey* is what you might get if you removed the plot from *Gormenghast* and crossed it with Ronald Firbank's *The Flower Beneath The Foot.* The result is a novel so abstruse and witty and disconnected from everything that it seems best to stumble from one page to the next and merely enjoy the juxtaposition of words.

On Dante, the Honourable Mr Listless says 'I find he is becoming fashionable, and I'm afraid I must read him some wet morning', before his companions launch into complaints that the reading public 'shun the solid food of reason for the light diet of fiction'. Then follows a long argument about writing and mermaids, ending with a song. It's that kind of book.

Crochet Castle, written thirteen years later, functions as a companion piece, and both lapse into theatrical dialogue packed with aphorisms when Peacock can't be bothered to scene-set anymore. His tales have no structure, thin characters, little human interest, and usually consist of people sitting around tables discussing the intellectual topics of the day, yet there's something here that can keep you reading. Peacock's books are a window to the past, and we feel we are eavesdropping on the kind of drunken, heady conversations English intellectuals have had in pubs for centuries.

After the death of his mother, the inconsolable author stopped writing for a quarter century, returning for a late finish before dying from injuries sustained in trying to save his library from a fire.

36. Elizabeth Jane Howard

Good authors get a few bites at the apple of fame; once for their debut novel, again when they're at the top of their game, and hopefully for a grand reprise when they're rediscovered by a new generation. Elizabeth Jane Howard's time is definitely back. Born in the 1920s, she grew up in a rather bohemian family (her father composed the music to 'Come Into The Garden, Maud') and became a model, then an actress, marrying Sir Peter Scott, the son of the explorer, at nineteen. Settling as a writer, she produced *The Beautiful Visit,* which won the John Llewellyn Rhys Prize in 1951, but only after a randy Jonathan Cape had brought a new meaning to the term 'publisher's advances'. It was followed by another six novels, short stories and a saga.

Those are the bare facts, but to get a true flavour of this time I'd recommend her racy and rather moving memoir *Slipstream*, a volume that proves a writer's life – especially a beautiful one – can be far from dull and sexless. Moving within literary circles, her third marriage was to Kingsley Amis, which says a lot about where the pursuit of love gets you, but she thought that if she got it right everything else would follow. One thing she did get right was the writing (she's a better prose stylist than Amis). Although it was fiction, her work drew heavily on biographical details. Her quartet of novels about a wartime family was filmed for TV as *The Cazalets*, but now her shorter pieces are enjoying a revival. The final haunting image of 'Three Miles Up' has stayed with me for years, and shows Howard's terrific storytelling strength. This and the eerie novella *Perfect Love*, about a tormented opera diva, were republished in a collection from Tartarus Press.

Howard's late novel *Falling* is an unnerving account of a sociopathic con-artist and his new prey, an ageing, vulnerable novelist to whom he craftily makes himself mentally and physically indispensable, and there's a temptation to read this as a bit of a *roman à clef.* Howard knows that there are mysterious pools of darkness in human nature, and leaves them in her elegant prose. These gaps allow room for argument and return you to her fiction. Now she has stepped out from behind the lights of the male authors who surrounded her to encourage fresh readers to her own individual work.

37. Rex Warner

'Important' books can sometimes be a chore, so here's a masterpiece with the pacing of a soap opera. The forgotten author of the Day-Lewis/Auden circle at Oxford in the 1920s, this dandyish vicar's son and disillusioned Marxist led a life packed with colour, incident, and by his own admission, lechery. After teaching in Egypt he returned home and produced his first novel, *The Wild Goose Chase*, in which three brothers stumble into a bizarre totalitarian kingdom. In *The Professor* he further explored the human cost of fascism as an academic is compromised and destroyed by life under a regime similar to that of Hitler's Germany.

Warner subsequently wrote propaganda films for the wartime Ministry of Information, then moved to Greece, producing historical novels and a translation of Thucydides' *History of the Peloponnesian War* that became a bestseller. He also returned to England after various amorous misadventures and remarried his ex-wife, but before all this he wrote *The Aerodrome.*

And what a perversely beautiful, horrific novel it is. Taking a contrary position to the prevailing attitude of the time (1941), that the British Air Force pilot represented a pinnacle of pure order in a time of dark chaos, *The Aerodrome* tells the story of Roy (clearly Rex), a young man at first fascinated and later repelled by the airmen whose sinister outpost slowly absorbs a lowly country village. Roy admires the ill-mannered Flight Lieutenant who casually offends villagers and steals his girl, because the pilots operate according to higher moral laws that place them far above the drunken, rowdy locals. But his respect proves misplaced; the Flight Lieutenant is a pen-pusher who has never flown, and as other secrets begin to tumble out, events are set in motion that lead to murder.

This vision of England has a clarity that descends directly from Dickens and Wilkie Collins. As Michael Moorcock says in his illuminating introduction to the new edition from Vintage Classics, 'there is something quietly and stubbornly confrontational in Warner which helps explain why he must periodically be rediscovered.'

Most mysterious of all is the order of importance Warner chooses for the book's sensational disclosures, so that the shooting of a mother in a crowded church or the adulterous betrayal of a friend is of little consequence in the pilots' minds, because they are merely an expedience on the path to higher glories. No wonder JG Ballard was such a fan.

38. Margery Allingham

I thought carefully about including Margery Allingham in this book. She's hardly ever out of print, and many readers know her name, even if they haven't read her. However, very few of them have really got to grips with her novels. The ones who have are passionate fans, and she has her own society which holds literary events throughout the year. For many years I had her wrongly pegged as an Agatha Christie knock-off, until I took time to properly read her prose.

What I discovered, and what I suspect everyone who becomes an Allingham fan discovers, is the extraordinary richness of her writing. It is allusive, colloquial, witty, bravura stuff – a window to a London mindset that is now so completely lost that it's sometimes best to have a copy of *Brewer's Phrase & Fable* beside your reading copy.

Allingham wrote her first crime novel in 1928 and continued for forty years. She regarded the mystery novel as a box with four sides: 'a killing, a mystery, an enquiry and a conclusion with an element of satisfaction in it.' She also distinguished between her 'right hand writing', which she did for pleasure, and her 'left hand writing', which was commissioned. Her detective was Albert Campion, aristocratic and unassuming to the point of vacancy, so ethereal that he vanishes altogether in the film version of her most famous novel. Campion is supported by the usual sidekick and cops (and unusually smart wife), but there any comparison to other crime writers must end, because Allingham is unique.

The first time I read *The Tiger In The Smoke*, the book widely regarded as her masterpiece, I kept losing my place. The chase to track Jack Havoc, jail-breaker and knife artist, in the London fog is as densely confusing as the choking gloom through which he carves his way. There's a central image of a hopping, running band of ragtag musicians silhouetted in the murk that stays beyond the conclusion. It's a dark, strange read and possibly not the best place to begin – but now, many of Allingham's books appear to have vanished into that pea-souper.

'I don't stick me 'ead into every nark's nest I 'ear of' says one character, and you want to hear the book read aloud, possibly by Sid James. Allingham's exuberant early prose gave way to a more mature, elegant style but both are wonderful. Her short fiction is easier to find, but less evocative.

39. Kyril Bonfiglioli

Imagine a politically incorrect combination of Bertie Wooster, Falstaff and Raffles, and you get an idea of this author's fictional hero. He appeared in (almost) four of Bonfiglioli's books, and is a wonderful invention. The author was born to an English mother and an Italian-Slovenian antiquarian book-selling father in Eastbourne, 1928. After 15 years as an art dealer in Oxford, an experience that clearly provided the background for his books, he became the editor of small science fiction magazines, although his own writings show little interest in that direction. All other biographical information about Bonfiglioli – that he was an expert swordsman, a good shot and a teetotaller, for example – is entirely wrong. Luckily, we now have his second wife's biography *The Mortdecai ABC* to thank for the facts (I seem to recall that she wrote to inform me that her husband's party piece was removing buttons with a sword).

Before his first book *Don't Point That Thing at Me* has even started, Bonfiglioli warns 'This is not an autobiographical novel. It is about some other portly, dissolute, immoral and middle-aged art dealer.' In fact, the first line is: 'When you burn an old carved and gilt picture frame it makes a muted hissing noise in the grate – a sort of genteel fooh – and the gold leaf tints the flames a wonderful peacock blue-green.' This is his snobbish, cowardly, dandy art thief Charlie Mortdecai speaking before fencing a Goya and attracting the murderous attention of several governments. Mortdecai is a delicious creation who, accompanied by his thuggish sidekick Jock, outrages the art world dullards of the 1970s as he heads towards come-uppance and a disgraceful cliffhanger of an ending.

Mortdecai returned (with no explanation whatsoever for the precipitous season-end interim) in *After You With The Pistol, Something Nasty In The Woodshed* and three-quarters of *The Great Mortdecai Moustache Mystery*, which was published posthumously, having been finished by the literary mimic Craig Brown, an act of forgery which Bonfiglioli would surely have adored.

His only other work is the hilarious *All The Tea In China*, which features a scurrilous Dutch ancestor of Mortdecai's. Everyone agrees that Bonfiglioli should have become world famous. The sad truth was that although his joyous books would have you believe otherwise, he lived in various states of poverty and alcoholism, and died of cirrhosis.

However, his wife Margaret told me that a friend of Kyril's, at the Gordon Highlanders Depot where they met, said her husband had taught him knife throwing, fencing and how to fry peas in Worcestershire sauce, so there's a real basis in the tall tales. She also pointed out that he could shoot a sixpence from the bravely held-out thumb and forefinger of a visiting French art dealer, standing at the far end of a large room.

Bonfiglioli's novels aren't ordinary enough to be simple crime capers; they're scabrous, witty, packed with demanding intelligent jokes, rude in the very best sense. He never found the right fans in his lifetime, but has become a true cult hero.

40. Hugh Wheeler

Some writers are forgotten because they are chameleons. Tracking their work becomes a slippery business. They change names, switch genres and merely leave behind their work, scattered through library systems and traceable only by their ISBN numbers. Throughout the process of researching these authors, one name remained on my to-do list from the outset. Hugh Callingham Wheeler was also known as Patrick Quentin, Jonathan Stagge and Q Patrick, and facts about him are hopelessly few, perhaps because he remained single and lived privately.

I do know that Wheeler was born in Hampstead, London in 1912 and died in 1987. He emigrated to America at the age of 22 and remained there all his life, spending twenty years writing almost forty novels. His *Puzzle* titled books became one of the best loved series in the US and several were produced as movies, including *Black Widow*, starring Van Heflin, Ginger Rogers and George Raft. It seems surprising that they have now vanished so completely.

However, Wheeler's greatest love was playwriting. His first production, *Big Fish, Little Fish*, starred Jason Robards and was directed by Sir John Gielgud. He was a man of easy wit who wrote for television and produced screenplays, including (with Jay Presson Allen) *Cabaret*, *Travels With My Aunt* and the hilarious *Black Flowers For The Bride*, starring Angela Lansbury as an imperious countess whose arrogant noble family is brought low, *Gormenghast*-style, by a social-climbing chauffeur.

Wheeler's award-winning work is still with us, though, because most of all he is remembered for his brilliant partnership with Stephen Sondheim, which produced adaptations and books for *A Little Night Music*, *Pacific Overtures* and *Sweeney Todd*. He also produced the book for Leonard Bernstein's hard-to-stage *Candide*.

Sweeney Todd appears to effortlessly capture the gloomy grotesqueries of the Victorian era. Wheeler opened the show with an immense front-drop of Cruikshank's etching of the British Beehive, showing the structure of the social classes within the empire. The play is harshly critical of the hypocrisies that could lead one man to elevation and another to penury. Sondheim remains a notorious perfectionist, reworking material again and again until he finds lasting forms, but perhaps he met his match in Wheeler, who enjoyed working beside such talented composers.

Wheeler also wrote new theatrical versions of *We Have Always Lived In The Castle* and *The Little Prince*. Unusually, he's an example of a writer who found longevity in collaboration rather than single authorship.

41. Richmal Crompton

Writers of children's books have to tread a fine line. They need their lead characters to be interesting and a little wayward, but if they're too wild the wrath of parents and librarians will be incurred. Too soft, and their target audience will lose interest.

Certain schoolboy heroes from the past have fallen from fashion, the victims of changing attitudes; the once hugely popular Billy Bunter books have been expunged from history, presumably for being calorifically challenged (I'd like to have covered Frank Richards' series but couldn't find any copies). Happily, several of Crompton's *Just William* books are available in reprint, although they are now a minority taste that probably appeals to older fans with a pronounced sense of nostalgia.

Most readers thought Richmal Crompton Lamburn was a man, and so shy was she that she did not disabuse them of the notion. The image of an anarchic, disruptive schoolboy shown with his cap askew and tie undone graced nearly forty volumes of exploits. Crompton wrote for adults too, but her lasting claim to fame is William Brown, whose adventures were populated with a gang of rebels called the Outlaws, including Ginger, Henry, Douglas and the awful, frilly, lisping Violet Elizabeth (catchphrase: 'I'm going to thcream and thcream until I'm thick!') who was appropriately played in a television adaptation by Bonnie Langford.

Crompton was born in Lancashire in 1890. The first William story appeared in *Home* magazine in 1919, and she continued writing them throughout her life, the last being published in 1970 after her death. There's something touching about a writer who never married producing books beloved by children. With a certain amount of boring inevitability, Crompton's books were later attacked by critics for being irrelevant and middle class, as if being able to write well was itself a liability. One reader points out that nowadays the books aren't a very easy read for preteens because they are peppered with words like 'epicurean', 'apoplectic' and 'discoursing', to which I say, 'Look it up'. And of course, William's rebelliousness – performing a conjuring trick with an egg that goes wrong, trying to arrange a marriage for his sister or planning to sell Ginger's twin brothers as slaves to raise money – is hopelessly mild compared to the minefield of text-bullying dangers facing modern parents. But perhaps an updated version, *William And The Crack Dealers*, featuring a schoolboy wielding a sharpened screwdriver instead of a catapult, might rob the books of their childhood charms.

42. Dr Christopher Evans

The more we behave like machines, they more they behave like us. Dr Christopher Evans was fascinated by this idea. He was a British computer scientist, experimental psychologist and writer, but to my mind his greatest claim to fame lies in two astonishing volumes he constructed with a highly unlikely assembly of authors.

Evans was born in Wales in 1931. He joined the National Physical Laboratory while in his twenties and wrote about a coming computer revolution, in which he predicted that microchips would transform world communications. The book, *Micro: The Impact Of The Computer Revolution* was successfully turned into a six-part TV series, but tragically Evans died before the book could be published and the series transmitted. The enemy of pseudoscience, Evans was also fascinated by the ways in which the human brain and its electronic equivalent might interact. Could computers replicate consciousness, and eventually learn to dream?

Authors appear to have a fascination with flying; indeed, it will become a recurring theme in this book. Evans was another passionate flyer and former RAF pilot whose thoughts turned to the links between man and machine. In 1969 these ideas coalesced into the anthology *Mind At Bay*, in which he suggested that the phantoms inhabiting our minds were about to take a new electronic form. The book gathers together eleven pieces complete with essays concerning our deepest hopes and fears. The stories are remarkable, covering everything from the fear of cancer, loneliness and going mad to the possibilities of the future and the likelihood that we would see an escalation of war in our lifetime. It comes as no surprise to find JG Ballard in the collection, writing about paranoia.

The book was a hit and spawned a sequel, *Mind In Chains.* This time, Evans explored an even more cerebral frontier, providing a virtual survival manual for the world to come. In it, he took several classic pieces by established authors and juxtaposed them with extreme experimental writing. Two electrifying pieces stand out. In *The Dreams Of The Computer* Evans sets out to confuse and disorientate a computer by deliberately misprogramming it. The computer eventually suffers a nervous breakdown and hallucinates. In *Anxietal Register B* John Sladek challenges the reader by providing a sinister form which must be filled in. The questions become increasingly intrusive, offensive and disturbing, and the form proves virtually impossible to complete.

Thanks to their appearance in ubiquitous paperback form, these touchstone volumes became unlikely bestsellers. They have never been reprinted.

43. Michael Green

Humour is an unrewarded genre; publishers like their fiction to have gravitas, which wins awards and looks important. Humour neither ages nor travels well, but part of every bestseller list consists of those slender joke volumes you see stacked by the checkout. There was once no getting away from Michael Green. His books were everywhere. The Leicester journalist, born 1927, was involved with amateur dramatics and enjoyed rugby, hobbies that inspired two guides, *The Art Of Coarse Acting* (also turned into a series of successful plays) and *The Art Of Coarse Rugby*. These bestsellers expanded to include other sports, and a very funny account of one man's battle to sell his house in *The Art Of Coarse Moving*. His biographical books included recollections of his press days, *Don't Print My Name Upside Down*, and the memoirs *The Boy Who Shot Down An Airship* and *Nobody Hurt In Small Earthquake*.

While Green is remembered as a fairly eccentric newspaperman who once started the printing presses to run off his own edition only to find that he couldn't stop them, nothing in his mild-mannered volumes quite prepares you for his classic, *Squire Haggard's Journal*, which, along with WE Bowman's *The Ascent Of The Rum Doodle*, is a one-of-a-kind volume that requires nothing more than a little knowledge of history and a sense of humour to appreciate.

The journal began as a series of columns and is a bawdy parody of a late 18th century gentleman's diary. Amos Haggard is a Hogarthian grotesque, chugging Madeira, horsewhipping servants, rogering prostitutes, evicting paupers and discharging his pistols at anything foreign. To avoid unpaid debts and an impending duel he flees the country, embarking on an unscheduled Grand Tour that allows him to behave in an indecent fashion toward the crowned heads of Europe. In the process, he reveals the origin of the Little Englander in all his sclerotic, xenophobic horror. The diary is obsessed with demises and unusual diagnoses, including 'Putrefaction Of The Tripes' and 'Death from Windy Spasms', and whether by accident or design somehow manages to capture the flavour of the times more succinctly than many carefully researched serious biographies.

When a writer is free to have fun with a topic the results sometimes yield pleasant surprises, and Squire Haggard is clearly a precursor to Blackadder. The book has been republished by Prion, who reissued a number of equally enjoyable humour classics.

44. John Dickson Carr

Sometimes authors simply fall out of favour with the public because they relentlessly pursue a single theme. Pennsylvania-born John Dickson Carr (1906-1977) hit upon the ultimate mystery, the murder that takes place in a hermetically sealed room, and wrote variations that increased in ornate complexity, with cliffhanger chapter ends and solutions that still have readers slapping their foreheads.

Writing prolifically under a number of pseudonyms including Carter Dickson, Carr became one of the greatest American writers of 'Golden Age' mysteries. Although his plots stretch credulity in the extreme, therein lies their great pleasure. His sleuth Dr Gideon Fell, fat and rumpled, with a cape, canes and monocle, was modelled on GK Chesterton, and Sir Henry Merrivale, blustery, noisy, Churchillian, is parodied in Anthony Schaffer's play *Sleuth*.

Sadly, we live in a time where there is no patience for barmy British sleuths who uncover insanely complex murders, and Dickson Carr wasn't remotely interested in offering his readers realism or relevance. Instead he provided cases that involved witchcraft, automata, eerie disappearances, snowstorms, impossible footprints, a hangman's ghost, corpses that walk through walls, a victim who dives into a swimming pool and vanishes. He combined an infectious joy with a powerful sense of the macabre, and once announced 'Let there be a spice of terror, of dark skies and evil things.'

After marrying an Englishwoman called Clarice Cleaves, he moved to England and produced a string of classics, including *The Judas Window*, in which he suggests that every room in London has a window only a murderer can see, and *The Hollow Man*, which involves a Transylvanian legend about being buried alive and is generally regarded as his greatest locked room mystery. A murderer kills his victim and literally vanishes, reappearing in the middle of an empty street to strike again, with watchers at either end who see nothing and no footprints appearing in freshly fallen snow. The book has a famously jaw-dropping double-plotted denouement.

Although he is regarded as a pulp writer, most of Carr's output possesses the graceful reliability of crafted clockwork. His writing is exotic, antiquarian, gruesome, steeped in Gothic imagery and yet filled with a sense of Wodehousian slapstick. In 1949 Carr had a great success with the authorised biography of Sir Arthur Conan Doyle, then turned to writing historical whodunits. He created legions of fans who have kept his name alive on the Internet, even if his books are as impossible to discover as the methods of his murderers.

45. Dorothy Bowers

Six letters, forgotten author starting with B.

Dorothy Bowers was a crossword compiler, born in Leominster, Herefordshire in 1902. She was the daughter of a bakery owner, and after a short and not especially joyful life died at 46 from tuberculosis. At least she had the satisfaction of knowing that she had just been inducted into the Detection Club, a society formed in 1930 by a group of Golden Age mystery writers that included Agatha Christie and GK Chesterton, and it seemed she might have gone on to greater things but for the ill-health that clearly affected her final novel.

After being one of the first women accepted at Oxford, Bowers struggled for several years to find a job as a history tutor, supplementing her meagre income by compiling her crossword puzzles. Keen to write, she found herself drawn to detective novels, but this was a career that usually attracted ladies of leisure.

Still, she quickly found her feet in the field. Her first novel, *Postscript To Poison*, was well received and inspired her to continue with the same leading characters, Inspector Dan Pardoe and Sergeant Salt, featuring in another three volumes.

According to Rue Morgue Press, who rescued her mysteries from obscurity, critics felt she might have gone on to succeed Dorothy L Sayers, but Bowers' time was occupied by her lowly teaching job and hampered by her delicate constitution. Her crime thrillers were championed by the press as 'fair play' mysteries where the clues are cunningly displayed within the context of the story, but in such a way that the reader is misdirected to disregard them.

Postscript To Poison features a hateful victim, Cornelia Lackland, who constantly changes her will and terrorises her two granddaughters before being dispatched by an unknown member of the household. *Shadows Before* also features a poisoning – in the tea, of course. Bowers' plots are intricate and her prose is thoughtfully crafted, with a certain amount of careful, eloquent wordplay integral to the solutions. If there's a criticism, it's that she coolly moves her characters like chess pieces, but this was a traditional approach in Golden Age crime. One of the most skilful wielders of the red herring, it's conceivable that Bowers would have gone on to produce a full body of work, for that is the best way to achieve a degree of artistic immortality.

46. Mary Renault

When men write about historical events, they tend to feed their readers facts and figures, but Mary Renault (1905-1983) was interested in the passions of the past. Her historical fiction was highly romantic, and here lies the key to her virtual disappearance from today's bookshelves. For many years Renault was a nurse in an Oxford brain surgery ward, and while working there she fell in love with a fellow nurse, Julie Mullard, with whom she remained all her life. Her early novels had contemporary settings, and when the fourth, *Return To Night*, won a sizeable cash prize, she and Julie emigrated to Durban, South Africa, which at the end of the 1940s had a more liberal attitude towards homosexuality than the British home counties.

In the next decade Renault spoke out against apartheid and produced her first openly gay romance. She had tackled the theme before, but in a more Platonic and oblique manner. The new book, *The Charioteer*, appeared in 1953 and described a love affair between two young servicemen in World War Two, but could not be published in the US because it was feared that readers would react with hostility to a serious gay love story.

Renault was drawn to romantic fiction but was anxious not to be labelled a gay writer. In the 1950s, the subject came with social and political issues attached, so she devised a way to express her fascination with the philosophical aspects of idealistic love by setting her novels in ancient Greece.

Despite her lack of classical training, she found herself able to recreate the period in vivid, muscular prose that presented her as an eyewitness to history. Over the next twenty-five years she produced a cycle of eight novels, starting with *The Last Of The Wine*, set in Athens during the Peloponnesian War, moving through the lives of Theseus, Plato, Dionysius and Alexander. In 1975 Renault produced her second non-fiction work, a biography of Alexander the Great. Ironically, her dedication to the politics of love was misinterpreted; feeling that passion had little to do with sexual orientation, she lost fans after expressing an antipathy with the nascent gay pride movement. She also managed to upset feminists by choosing to write about the world of powerful men. This is a tragedy, because her books have stood the test of time and deserve better treatment. *Fire From Heaven* is a good place to start.

47. Nevil Shute & Eric Ambler

While neither of these classic authors is truly forgotten, their words have faded to a faintness only discerned by loyal fans. Reprints are available and second-hand copies lie in Oxfam shops, but both have been caught out by the passage of time.

Neville Shute wrote wartime aircraft adventures and Eric Ambler produced sophisticated Europe-set 1930s thrillers, but what links them (apart from the fact that their paperbacks tended to sit side by side on second-hand bookshelves) is their ability to tell 20th century stories filled with enthralling action sequences and characters you care about, linking events into larger political settings. This basic storytelling skill lately seems to have become buried within vast self-important volumes, so it's a shock to note the brevity of most Shute and Ambler novels. Like their heroes and heroines, the authors get in, do the job well and get out.

Nevil Shute's actual surname was Norway. Like many writers in the twenties and thirties, he was fascinated by flying, so his heroes are often independent pilots. In the fifties, he switched his locations to Australia and wrote his two most famous books, the post-apocalyptic *On The Beach* and *A Town Like Alice*, in which a young Englishwoman and an Australian cattleman survive starvation and torture during the war in Malaya, and later found a new outback town. Uncomplicated novels about fundamentally good people are unfashionable now, and Shute has become a minority taste.

Ambler came from a London music hall family and toured as a comic, but became more politically aware than the Oxford-educated Shute. A committed anti-fascist, his novels reflected the growing ideological complexity of his time, and his taut thrillers, like *The Mask Of Dimitrios* and *Journey Into Fear,* came early in his career. His heroes often get out of their depth in the cynical, murky world of European espionage. 'What else could you expect from a balance of power', asks one of his characters, 'adjusted in terms of land, of arms, of man-power and of materials: in terms, in other words, of money?'

A later novel, *The Light Of Day*, adopted a lighter tone and concerned jewel thieves trying to rob the Istanbul museum. It was filmed as *Topkapi* and subsequently parodied in *The Pink Panther*. Ambler moved to Hollywood and scripted *The Cruel Sea* which secured an Oscar nomination, and *A Night To Remember*, about the sinking of the Titanic. The Shute and Ambler paperbacks have evocative covers and have become collectable of late.

48. Gary Indiana

Some authors are less forgotten than ignored. Gary Indiana is an author it's more convenient to overlook. He belongs to a special breed of American urban writers who take cool pleasure in dissecting the lives of the rich and ugly, and is possibly the most jaded chronicler of them all. On a good day he makes Bret Easton Ellis look like Enid Blyton, and yet many, myself included, think he might already have written the Great American Novel.

Indiana was an actor before working at New York's influential *Village Voice* as an art critic. He became an essayist and journalist, and wrote non-fiction on cultural phenomena, from Pasolini to Warhol and Schwarzenegger. However, his first love is the satirical novel. A loose trilogy lightly fictionalised criminal cases and their accompanying media frenzies; *Three Month Fever* follows the disintegrating personality of Gianni Versace's murderer in Miami and the grotesque sensationalism of its press coverage. *Resentment* is a work of angry genius based on the circus following the trial of the Menendez brothers, wealthy Californians who killed their parents and left a screenplay version of events on their computer. *Depraved Indifference* explores more charismatic sociopathy, as a pathetic heiress is killed by mother-and-son confidence tricksters. Indiana's language is precise, literate, painfully honest and shockingly funny. He bravely surfs through the 20th century's end-times with a reptilian eye that watches who gets to eat and who is eaten. His characters are disappointed with their share of American dream, and become slowly poisoned by it.

But there is a problem – clearly, there has to be otherwise the author would be as feted as Don DeLillo or Tom Wolfe – Indiana is as detested as he is adored, for his all-encompassing cynicism, his cruelties, his refusal to sentimentalise, his immense vocabulary, his stylistic inconsistencies. He is addicted to the world that repels him so much, but moments of tenderness seep through the cracks. When he describes a conversation with his mother or the sadness of fading glamour he seems a direct descendant of Truman Capote or Tennessee Williams. A later book, *The Shanghai Gesture*, is a bizarre take on Fu Manchu, the opening sentence being 'Among Those That Know, a cabal our story will elucidate in the fullness of time, rumours fluttered that Dr Obregon Petrie defied the laws of gravity when it suited his caprice.' It's not typical of his work, but it's great fun.

49. Winifred Watson

When it comes to literary success, timing is everything. Before JK Rowling's boy wizard there had been a virtual industry of magic-schoolboy tales, but Harry Potter was the one that clicked. Winifred Watson's literary career was curtailed by three major events: the Depression, the attack on Pearl Harbor and the Blitz.

Watson was born in 1906 in Newcastle upon Tyne, and remained there all her life. Due to follow her sisters into higher education, she found the way blocked when her father's shoe shops failed in the Depression of 1929. She wrote her first book, the Northumbrian historical drama *Fell Top*, in dull days stuck behind a secretarial desk, after her boss suggested bringing in knitting to keep herself amused. Finishing it in six weeks, she stuck it in a drawer and forgot about it until spotting an advert from Methuen looking for new writers. The novel was critically well-received and became a radio play. Watson was young and pretty, and got local coverage, so the publishers asked her for more. The result was *Odd Shoes*, produced in a different style that benefitted from proper research.

Her third book horrified Methuen. Instead of being serious it was fun, and she was writing on subjects she knew nothing about. The book was *Miss Pettigrew Lives For A Day*, about a frumpy governess who is accidentally sent by her agency to work for a louche actress and night club singer running a complicated love life. Watson said 'I didn't know anyone like Miss Pettigrew. I just made it all up. I haven't the faintest idea what governesses really do. I've never been to a nightclub and I certainly didn't know anyone who took cocaine.'

The book was an immediate hit with the public, and a Hollywood musical was planned starring Billie Burke, the good witch from *The Wizard Of Oz*. The bombing of Pearl Harbor put paid to that. 'I wish the Japanese had waited six months', she said later.

Watson married and wrote every day, but when the house next door was blown up in the war, her family was forced to move into one room with her parents, making writing impossible. Persephone Books persevered with the republication of *Miss Pettigrew Lives For A Day*, and the book found its way onto Hollywood desks once more. A rather charming film version starring Frances McDormand and Amy Adams finally appeared six years after Watson's death.

50. Luis Van Rooten

Every Christmas the shops are flooded with gift books based on TV shows, wartime hobbies and compendia of schoolboy knowledge played for ironic laughs. Who would have thought there was money to be made from clipping children's pastimes out of the *Arthur Mee Children's Encyclopædiae*? Christmas wasn't always a cue to make money from old rope, though. In the past there had been some inspired comic volumes, and it's a pleasure to see that Luis Ricardo Carlos Fernand d'Antin y Zuloaga van Rooten's masterpiece is back in bookstores each December.

Who, you say? Luis was a popular multilingual actor, born in 1906 in Mexico, whose father worked for the American Embassy and was assassinated in a railway compartment because 'he knew too much'. His son trained as an architect, then moved to Hollywood to become a radio announcer. Because he had a velvety accent and looked a bit swarthy, he began to land Mephistophelian movie roles, playing Heinrich Himmler at both ends of his career, and appearing as a villain opposite everyone from Kirk Douglas to Edward G Robinson. He voiced leading roles in Disney's *Cinderella*, and was also a skilled designer, horticulturalist and artist before his interest in language turned him to writing.

His sophisticated humour books include *Van Rooten's Book Of Improbable Saints*, but he should be remembered for creating a slim volume in 1967 that has become a perennial classic, the unique trick book *Mots D'Heures: Gousses, Rhames: The D'Antin Manuscript*. To the untutored eye it appears to be a dry annotated volume of obscure French poetry, complete with mediaeval woodcuts. The best way to give it to someone is not to tell them anything about it, and wait for the penny to drop. For this is a rare example of homophonic translation, a literary device that renders a text in one language to its pronunciation into another with an entirely different meaning. Opening the pages to one poem we find:

Un petit d'un petit
S'étonne aux Halles
Un petit d'un petit
Ah! degrés te fallent

Because of course, the book's phonetic title is *Mother Goose Rhymes*, and those four lines introduce us to Humpty Dumpty. Luis then annotates the passage to explain the new meaning of the poem, thus rendering the translation into twisted, hilariously pseudo-philosophical gibberish. Remember to take the wraparound cover off if you buy it, as the most recent editions have stupidly given the game away on the front.

Maryann Forrest

HERE

(away from it all)

"SHE KNOCKS ME OUT COMPLETELY – she's a stunning writer! Such imagination, humanity and wit . . . so superb and alive a talent"
TIME OUT

MAYFLOWER

583 11995 6
2

The Man Who
Held the Queen
to Ransom and
Sent Parliament
Packing
Peter Van
Greenaway

BOOK SOCIETY CHOICE

The Provincial Lady in War-Time

E. M. Delafield

Illustrated by Illingworth

CHRISTIE MALRY'S OWN DOUBLE-ENTRY

B. S. JOHNSON

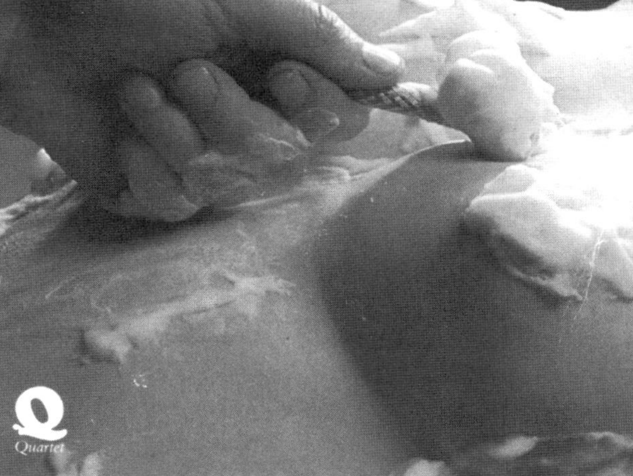

"Undoubtedly the funniest book
I've ever read" Jack Benny
THE HORSE
IS DEAD
Robert Klane

Panther Horror

Mind in Chains

Edited by
Dr. Christopher Evans

Stories of horror
from the skull's
unmapped
depths

Panther

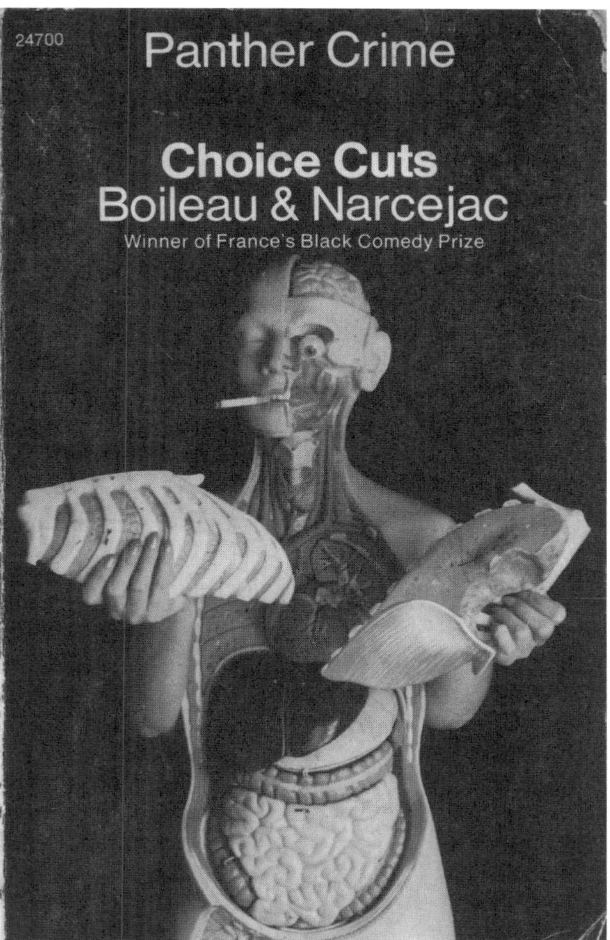
24700
Panther Crime
Choice Cuts
Boileau & Narcejac
Winner of France's Black Comedy Prize

HOW TO BE TOPP

Geoffrey Willans and
Ronald Searle

51. Richard Hughes

Hughes first came to public attention at 17 when his schoolmaster sent one of his essays to *The Spectator*. He wrote the world's first radio play, called *Danger*, broadcast in 1924. He became a journalist, travelled extensively, married the painter Frances Bazley, and spent a decade as a scriptwriter at Ealing Studios, but only managed to write four adult novels, two of which have ostensibly similar plots.

This is odd, because one of the quartet has such timeless power that it should probably be on every school curriculum. *A High Wind In Jamaica* was published to great acclaim in 1929, and is quite unique. It is an adventure about children, but is not aimed at them. The prose sweeps away a century of Victorian sentimentality and replaces it with something darker, more clear-eyed and modern.

What starts as merely masterful storytelling becomes something dreamlike and haunting; it's not a book you easily forget. The first page sets the tone when it casually mentions that twin sisters were starved and fed ground glass until they died. Some British children living in Jamaica survive a hurricane and are sent back to England, but are captured by pirates. The description of the storm is filled with bizarre incident – a pack of wildcats is blown through the windows onto the dining table, and the shutters bulge 'as if tired elephants were leaning against them'.

It's a book about growing up and recognising the cruelties that allow the young to survive. Nothing fazes the children, whose amoral attitude to their parents should be a warning that the pirates are not psychologically matched to defeat them. The plot turns on a casually shocking death that underlines the loss of innocence they suffer. Hughes is brilliant at pinning down the interior lives of children, and it would be interesting to know how today's kids react to it.

Hughes's other seabound novel, *In Hazard*, feels like a spin-off, as it follows the crew of a British ship facing death in a hurricane. It's thrilling, but much less memorable. Two further books outline a virtual history of the early 20th century, but are patchy. Hughes was given the OBE, and died fifty pages into the last volume in the trilogy. Vintage Classics are to be commended for their editions of *A High Wind In Jamaica* and *In Hazard*, but the others – and his excellent children's stories – are out of print.

52. William Fryer Harvey

Looking back at the lives of these authors, it seems that the fastest way to become forgotten is to be compared to some of the century's greatest writers. In 1955, *The Times Literary Supplement* praised William Fryer Harvey as the equal of MR James and Walter De La Mare, at which point he started a decline into such obscurity that even the Internet is of little help in locating his fiction.

Harvey was feted for saving lives in an ambulance unit in World War One, but the Leeds-born Quaker should be remembered as one of Britain's finest ghost story writers. Many literary giants have turned their hands to this genre, and as a consequence it's difficult to make a mark in a crowded field, but Harvey's style feels like a dark shadow-image to the tales of Saki, and deserves to be celebrated.

Having sustained lung damage in the war, Harvey remained in poor health throughout his relatively brief life (he died at 52), and took up writing short fiction that employed the irrational subconscious to powerful effect. Although his output was fairly small, his stories benefitted from their lack of easy conclusion and modern psychological insight. I count nine collections, but several have overlapping stories, and all are out of print. His best tales include the gruesome school yarn 'The Dabblers', and 'The Man Who Hated Aspidistras'.

In 1928 Harvey published 'The Beast With Five Fingers', which was filmed nearly two decades later with Peter Lorre in the lead. 'The hand was writhing in agonised contortions, squirming and wriggling upon the nail like a worm upon a hook', he wrote, in this acclaimed tale of a pianist whose severed hand returns from his mausoleum to stage vengeful attacks on his secretary, who secretly craves the dead man's fortune. The film was a big hit, partly because of its exemplary special effects. Luis Buñuel is rumoured to have had a part in their design, and the surreal sight of the hand scuttling up a piano keyboard suggests this was so. The film also boasted music by Max Steiner, and retains much of its strange, haunting power. It led to a renewed interest in Harvey's work, and a few reprints followed.

Recently, Tartarus Press published his complete short stories under the title *The Double Eye*, so it's now possible to plug another gap in the century's roll-call of top short fiction writers.

53. Julia O'Faolain

It would have been more surprising if Julia O'Faolain hadn't become a writer; born in 1932, she was the daughter of two successful authors. Her father was Sean O'Faolain, an Irish short story writer who fought for the Republicans during the Irish civil war, and made bombs which her mother smuggled for the IRA. He was also made the *Saoi* of *Aosdána*, the highest honour in Ireland for the Arts. Julia studied in Rome and Paris, and her brilliant fiction reflects both influences. *Godded and Codded* (also published as *Three Lovers*) is a fairly raucous comedy concerning the Irish virgin's dilemma, taking the form of sexual adventures in Paris. It's the tale of an innocent abroad, with a few nice digs at Irish ex-pats. When the inevitably pregnant heroine returns to her family in Ireland we come to a better understanding of her wild behaviour.

Her novel *No Country for Young Men* was set in Dublin, and traces three generations in a variety of narrative threads; it's her best book, and was shortlisted for the Booker prize in 1980. Her works are strongly influenced by Irish identity. In *We Might See Sights!* O'Faolain used her homeland as the setting for several stories satirising sexual repression. Her other short-story collections include *Man in the Cellar*, *Melancholy Baby*, and *Daughters of Passion*.

O'Faolain writes about women's roles in society, power, faith and sexuality, and about Irish dilemmas of female identity. *Women In The Wall* is a history of Queen Radegund, who in the 6th century founded a monastery in Gaul. With her husband, she edited *Not in God's Image: Women in History from the Greeks to the Victorians*, and produced a new novel, *Adam Gould*, set in a lunatic asylum. Although it was her first book in 17 years, it explored familiar themes: clerical intrigue, family history and farce, with madness added to the mix. She said 'I like fiction to be a Trojan horse. It can seem to be engineering an escape from alien realities, but its true aim is to slip inside them and get their measure.' O'Faolain is a wonderful stylist and an exciting writer, which makes it all the more surprising that she is often overlooked. Her work is joyous, urbane and intensely Irish. Although that last book is still in print, the rest are – you guessed it – hard to find now.

54. BS Johnson

We had to reach him sooner or later. For several decades Johnson was the ultimate forgotten author, born in 1933, dead at 40, beloved by critics, overlooked by the public. He didn't write much; seven slender novels of increasing peculiarity, a handful of plays and short stories, but they were enough to set him at the forefront of the British *avant garde*. He was an unashamed experimentalist frustrated by linear storytelling, who rejected the Dickensian limitations of the novel, earning the gratitude of Anthony Burgess and the enmity of Peter Ackroyd. Perhaps he was born too early; he would have loved the playfulness of the Internet, although his writing might well have been destroyed by it.

I first encountered Johnson's work in my late teens, in *Christie Malry's Own Double-Entry* (with its gratuitous cover of a man shaving a woman's breasts). The book, at just 115 pages, was entrancing and annoying in equal measure; Malry works in a bank and attempts to run his life on a bookkeeping system, but soon discovers that life debits far more than it credits, and must increasingly resort to acts of terrorism in order to keep his account in balance. To clear his debts he poisons half of Hammersmith, but life takes revenge in the form of cancer. It was a high concept idea to fall in love with, badly served by a belated film version that at least sported an appropriate level of perversity.

House Mother Normal described a bizarre social evening in an old people's home from the perspectives of the eight inhabitants, in decreasing order of their lucidity. It's still shocking, typographically brave and finally moving. *The Unfortunates* is his infamous 'book in a box', its chapters presented unbound so that the reader can choose them in any order. Beneath this, it's a fairly straightforward meditation on death and friendship, told through memories. *Albert Angelo* has a hole cut in some pages that reveal a future event in the book.

As interested in typography and the use of blank spaces as he was in words, Johnson is utterly unique, a product of the self-indulgent sixties perhaps, but we need to be tested by such writers. His collection *Aren't You Rather Young To Be Writing Your Memoirs?* is poetic, passionate and strangely conversational. He wrote about and filmed his own life, and like Joe Orton, we will always wonder where he would have gone next.

Four of Johnson's novels have been reprinted, but best of all is Jonathan Coe's miraculous biography *Like A Fiery Elephant*, which replicates his idiosyncratic style while illuminating his short life.

55. Francis Durbridge

I suspect there are readers who not only remember Durbridge's work but who can also whistle his theme tune, which was either *Coronation Scot* by Vivian Ellis, or Rimsky-Korsakov's *Scheherazade*, depending on your age.

The Hull-born author and playwright was born in 1912 and died in 1998. His output was prodigious; I count at least thirty five novels, twenty-two TV series, seven theatrical plays and around thirty radio plays and serials. He sold his first play to the BBC at 21, and created his most enduring character, the crime novelist/detective Paul Temple, at 26. In many ways he was the first of the popular multi-media writers, with simultaneous hits on radio, TV, film and in print. In later life he turned to the theatre with similar success. Typically, the critics sneered and the public adored him. Now, his books have completely vanished and only some of his radio plays survive, kept alive by the BBC's desire to turn a buck and make up for wiping much of their archives.

Durbridge also used the pen name of Paul Temple, thus becoming his own character. There's a warm glow of nostalgia around his middle-class mysteries, which usually turn on the elaborate planning and solution of a murder, with plenty of cliff-hangers. He was less interested in the whodunit so much as the will-he-get-away-with-it? because he knew this was a better way to create suspense.

But are the stories any good? Actually yes; I think of him as the English Cornell Woolrich, a pulp fiction writer whose energetic style contrasted with the enervating period in which he wrote. Paul Temple is absurdly British, rather too solid and square-jawed for most people to take seriously, but he proved instantly popular and went on to become one of the most successful characters ever created for broadcasting, which makes his disappearance strange.

Our detectives are more complex and beset with personal problems now. Temple's world is filled with lost images; it's a world of telephone exchanges, manor houses, glamorous cabaret artists, Mayfair flats, mysterious piano tuners, diamond robberies, kidnaps, clergymen and calling cards, where carrier pigeons are used to smuggle gems and the only clue to a crime is a cocktail stick. It's easy to make fun of such plots – and why not? *The 39 Steps* became a huge hit again on the London stage by doing just that – but it's a shame that his thrillers disappeared so completely. Be heartened, though, as a few of his best books have lately been reprinted.

56. Bram Stoker

Of course he wrote *that* book, but Abraham Stoker (1847-1912) wrote fifteen others besides. Nearly all of his output appears to have vanished, eclipsed by the novel with which he will ever be associated. Admittedly no-one now will want to thumb through *The Duties of Clerks of Petty Sessions In Ireland*, but there are other works that share common themes with *Dracula.* Given the immense success of the novel that influences a vast body of work about vampires, from the drippy *Twilight* to the brilliant *Let The Right One In*, you'd think anything that enlightens us further would be readily available.

Whether 'Dracula's Guest' was actually excised from the novel or not, it serves as an excellent curtain-raiser. In this, an unnamed Englishman survives an encounter with an undead countess in a graveyard (she's handily despatched with a bolt of lightning), only to be summoned by the count to his castle. The story was always found heading up collections of Stoker's short fiction.

Much has been made of the author's early childhood sickliness, and the way in which it created an interest in supernatural fiction, but a glance at his other novels reveals that Stoker was capable of inventing a range of occult tropes, from the disturbing blanched creature that rears its head in *The Lair Of The White Worm*, to his mummy-revivification tale, *The Jewel Of The Seven Stars*, which had its original grisly ending lopped off and replaced with something more upbeat.

The Lady Of The Shroud starts brilliantly, with what appears to be a female vampire in a floating coffin, but transforms into a painfully turgid tale of Balkan nationalism. More interesting are Stoker's fairy tales, like 'How Seven Went Mad' and 'The Invisible Giant', and the supernatural stories, the best of which is the palpable evil of 'The Judge's House'. Some of Stoker's short fiction remains uncollected. The author did not visit the Eastern Europe outlined in his imagination but chose instead to befriend America, where *Dracula* was transformed through film into one of the 20th century's most enduring fables.

And here, perhaps, is another reason why authors' works are left behind. Thanks to its endless reinventions on film, *Dracula* has a timeless visual appeal that his other works now lack, so the intriguing collection *Snowbound: The Record Of A Theatrical Touring Party*, has completely disappeared, while *Dracula*, like its titular character, lives on.

57. Kathleen Winsor

Authors are prone to notoriety. Any printed display of opinion is bound to raise questions, and then there's the matter of censorship. In this case, censorship in America – something Kathleen Winsor (1919-2003) discovered the hard way. Winsor was a smart, energetic sports columnist who subsequently became fascinated by the Restoration period. After years of research she produced a sprawling fifth draft of her first novel that topped out at around 2,500 pages. Her publishers hacked it down to a more manageable size, just under a thousand pages, and it appeared in 1944 as *Forever Amber*. The novel was a love letter to London, a bodice-ripping romp through plague and fire, taking in the society chatter and politics of the times. There were a few mildly titillating passages, and the book was generally well received by critics who saw parallels between the enduring Restoration wives and their wartime counterparts. It didn't hurt that the attractive author, then 24, was seductively photographed for her press releases.

No-one had foreseen that the book would be banned. When the Massachusetts attorney-general cast a magnifying glass over the text he found more than seventy references to sexual intercourse and ten scenes in which women undressed in front of men. Critics grimly accused the book of glorifying the superficial life of a courtesan. State after state followed suit, blocking the blockbuster and pronouncing it pornography, and soon Winsor found she had created a national scandal. Naturally, it became the bestselling novel of the 1940s, and was transformed into a pretty dreadful Otto Preminger film, bowdlerised by the Catholic League of Decency to include an ending in which the heroine is punished for her sins.

Winsor's only sin was to write something that was sexy and fun in a time of finger-wagging conservatism. Instead of wartime austerity, she offered something more appealing, notoriously announcing that 'Adultery is not a crime, it's an amusement.'

Scandal and success combined to destroy Winsor's marriage. She wedded the band leader Artie Shaw, and when that relationship failed she married her divorce attorney. In her next novel, *Star Money*, she wrote a thinly disguised biography about becoming a bestselling author, but despite being billed as the new fiction from the author of *Forever Amber*, it was received with indifference. The moment had passed. Winsor continued to write until 1986, but none of her fiction made any impact. It can fairly be said that the success of her first novel upset the balance of her life.

58. Lionel Davidson

He's another of those authors who turns up a lot on the racks of second-hand bookshops, in sexy little Penguin editions that fit a pocket. A Yorkshireman who spent years as a freelance reporter, Davidson's versatile, pacy novels propelled him into the forefront of thriller writing. Although they are now back in print, mentioning his name to younger readers produces blank looks. Let's put that right; he's a terrific writer. His first novel, *The Night Of Wenceslas*, concerns a young spendthrift forced into a spying trip to Prague during the Cold War, in order to retain his beloved car (used as a stake in his debts). Our anti-hero manages to get beaten up before flushing the information down the toilet, and falls deep into a trap of his own making. It's a typical Davidson ploy, to graft a sympathetic character into an increasingly elaborate plot.

His second novel, *The Rose Of Tibet*, had something of H Rider Haggard about it, and was a genuine adventure that won the admiration of Graham Greene and Daphne Du Maurier. This tale of a quest for treasure from India to Tibet should, by rights, have been a Harrison Ford film. I first discovered Davidson in *Smith's Gazelle*, and being of an impressionable age, was moved to tears. It's a fable concerning a small Jewish boy and a wizened old Arab who join forces during the Six Day War to save the titular gazelle (the last of its species) from extinction. The story has a wonderful timelessness and a compelling message.

The Chelsea Murders won Davidson the Gold Dagger Award for best thriller. It presents a chillingly disguised murderer and a raft of memorably louche Chelsea characters, although the plot favours method over motive a little too much. It also poses a common problem with books from the 1970s: a lack of political correctness that simply reflected the attitudes of the time, which is no direct fault of the author's.

Davidson's later thriller, *Kolymsky Heights* (1994), has a terrific premise. The hero is a Canadian-Indian with a linguistic talent that allows him to infiltrate one of the most forbidding places on earth, a secret laboratory buried deep in the permafrost of Siberia. The question is not just whether he'll succeed in his mission, but how he'll ever get out. As usual, the style and pacing of the story is superb.

59. Michael McDowell

'I am a commercial writer and I'm proud of that', said Alabama-born Michael McDowell, 'I think it is a mistake to try to write for the ages.' His Gothic Deep South novels appeared mainly as paperbacks in the golden age of the throwaway read, the early 1980s, but there's something about them that remains to haunt the reader. McDowell earned high praise and good sales, producing some thirty volumes including mysteries, comedies, period adventures, psychological suspensers and family epics. He also adopted aliases for two sets of pastiche novels, one featuring a gay detective. Pointedly hailed by Stephen King as 'a writer for the ages', his prose was tight and his idiomatic dialogue was shorn of folksiness.

McDowell frequently returned to the idea of matriarchal revenge in his books, and his wonderfully conversational style made it feel as if he was imparting a terrible piece of gossip while describing all manner of disturbing events. It is generally accepted that his best book was *The Elementals*, in which two families fatefully clash during a summer holiday on a spit of land being slowly engulfed by tides and mournful spirits.

Personally, I prefer his six-volume *Blackwater* saga, which chronicles a tragic fifty year period in the lives of the Caskey family, whose women bear a strange affinity for water in all forms, and whose vengeance knows no bounds. The saga plays out like a gruesomely overheated Dickensian soap with fantastical overtones and outrageous cliffhangers, and is constructed for maximum page-turning efficiency. They also say something about the South's preoccupation with breaking levees and inundation. Surely they're ripe for republication?

Cold Moon Over Babylon is set in the harvest season of a foggy Southern town, and has a marvelous feel for its location. McDowell frequently returns to the idea of being engulfed by natural forces, as man-made walls collapse and seas rise (in *The Elementals* sand pours in through the windows of an abandoned house) and he links these natural catastrophes to our own selfishness or blindness, flaws that leave dark stains on future generations. His characters are often powerless and insignificant in the face of time and nature.

McDowell was a creator of highly visual images, and wrote the classic comedy *Beetlejuice*, also collaborating on *The Nightmare Before Christmas*. Even when outlining horrific acts, there's a gentility and grace to McDowell's prose. He died shortly before his fiftieth birthday. All of his books are out of print, although I recently spotted four volumes of *Blackwater* in a secondhand bookshop in Brighton.

60. Mazo de la Roche

A favourite game is to ask friends to name their own *Invisible Ink* writer, and here's one that came up time and again. Mazo de la Roche was a prolific Victorian Canadian, born 1879 in Ontario, who became the author of a popular series of novels, and remains a Canadian icon, but her books are almost unknown in the UK. Roche was a lonely and often unwell child, the daughter of a struggling salesman, and like many children in similar situations she became the creator of a rich fantasy world. In Roche's case, however, this world was populated and coloured in a detailed, complex vision that led her, belatedly, to write romantic fiction.

Her first two efforts fared poorly, but her talent was soon recognised. When her third novel, *Jalna*, won a valuable *Atlantic Monthly* literary prize, she realised her dream (at the age of 48) and began to expand upon her fantasy world of rural aristocracy. *Jalna* became one of the greatest romantic bestsellers of its time, and was extended into a set of 16 novels also known as *The Whiteoak Chronicles*, which covered a century of family life. Roche took her characters' names from gravestones, but their story was her own writ large, with the recurring theme of a frequently unemployed father, a sick mother and an orphaned cousin brought to safety and stability by the anchor of a family home. In reality Roche lived reclusively with her younger cousin and raised two children with her, finding happiness here and in her books after a difficult, crowded and impoverished start in life.

The *Jalna* books became a Hollywood movie, a play and a television series. They were so successful that Roche expanded her vision, delving further back into the history of the household to give her readers more background to the tribulations of the Whiteoak family.

In Britain the *Jalna* books were issued by Pan with classic romance covers, usually depicting a headstrong, windswept girl collapsing into the muscular arms of a fit chap with an aristocratic jaw. The books were less popular in their native land than in Europe and America, mainly because Canadians found little of their country reflected in the stories, which followed a European tradition of romantic wish-fulfilment.

A late lapse into sentiment and formula resulted in Roche's loss of popularity, but now she is considered to be a national treasure in her homeland.

61. John Collier

For those of a certain age, John Collier was simply 'the window to watch', as the TV commercials for the menswear store proclaimed. The other John Collier is far more interesting, an English writer, born 1901, who became famous for his wonderful short stories. Setting out to be a poet, Collier was disappointed with the result and instead produced a strange novel, *His Monkey Wife*, a satire about an explorer who marries a chimpanzee. Two more novels followed, now both forgotten, but around them formed a body of uniquely sardonic short stories, often written for *The New Yorker* magazine. They were collected in many volumes, one of which, *Fancies And Goodnights*, was reprinted in 2003.

In some ways, Collier feels like a natural successor to Saki. His simple, sharp style brought his tales colourfully to life with a hint of brimstone. 'The Devil George And Rosie' starts 'There was a young man who was invariably spurned by the girls, not because he smelt at all bad but because he happened to be as ugly as a monkey.'

In his most famous story, 'Evening Primrose', a failed poet bids the world farewell and moves into a department store, only to find that others have also moved there to escape the world. It was filmed for television as a Stephen Sondheim musical in 1966. Another story, 'Green Thoughts', about a man-eating plant, became the basis for the film *Little Shop Of Horrors*, also made into a musical.

Collier was married to a silent movie actress and moved to Los Angeles, where he contributed to many films and TV shows. His tales often had a fantastical element, and some were adapted for *Alfred Hitchcock Presents*, a format they fitted perfectly. He contributed to screenplays for *The African Queen*, and *I Am A Camera*, the basis for *Cabaret*, but within a decade of working in Hollywood, his output – typically – became much less original and interesting.

Collier was his own harshest critic, and once said 'I sometimes marvel that a third-rate writer like me has been able to palm himself off as a second-rate writer', but there is no-one quite like him. In 1972, *The John Collier Reader*, a collection of almost fifty first-rate stories selected by the author, was published to fresh acclaim. How could you not love an author who writes a story entitled 'Night! Youth! Paris! and the Moon!' Perhaps because he is so unclassifiable, Collier's books have all but vanished.

62. HRF Keating

The ebullient Mr Keating wrote around sixty novels, but now he – and too many other good senior authors – are hard to spot on bookshelves groaning with endless volumes of *Do Penguins Have Ears?*, so warrants this inclusion. Henry Reymond Fitzwalter Keating was born in 1926 near Hastings, and is the author of twenty-four Inspector Ghote mysteries, which are set in the old offices of the Bombay CID. Keating did not visit India until a full decade and nine novels had passed – proof that you don't always need to write from experience. He actually felt that the books were harder to write after his visit. His other recurring characters were tough DCI Harriet Marten, and charlady Mrs Craggs, who appeared in a number of short stories.

In the same way that you can watch a 1960s film and be less fascinated by the plot than the art direction, so Keating's early whodunits work well as social documents – although that's not to dismiss their plots, which often feature excellent twists.

In his police procedural *Is Skin Deep, Is Fatal* from 1965, a police superintendent investigates the gassing of a night club tart, and although the narrative features a plot clue that virtually pokes you in the eye with a stick, it's a terrific snapshot of the flyblown Soho nightlife that was still untouched by any sign of Swinging London. This is a world where secretaries know more about their bosses than wives, everyone makes smutty remarks and hints at sex, but no-one manages to live out their fantasies. When faced with a gaggle of beauty queens at a murder site, Keating's cop 'brought order like a sedulous botanist in a wild garden.' As with so many of the more experienced authors, his language is rich and succinct.

With virtually no technology to call upon, Keating's dogged officers of the law carried out their work the old-fashioned way, by getting to know the neighbourhood, unravelling red tape and keeping tabs on troublemakers. Keating has a natural ear for dialogue, and his banter moves the action forward at a decent pace.

Keating also produced the definitive biography of Agatha Christie and other volumes that greatly add to our knowledge of crime fiction, including a crime-lovers' bible entitled *Whodunit*. Keating won the crime writers' holy grail of awards, the Gold Dagger, for his book *The Perfect Murder*, and quite rightly too.

63. William Haggard

James Bond has a lot to answer for. At the height of Bond Mania, in the mid-1960s, a number of other espionage writers emerged, some as good or better than 007's painfully snobbish creator. One of these, described rather damningly by the *Sunday Express* as 'the adults' Ian Fleming', was William Haggard, the pseudonym of Richard Clayton. He produced some thirty three novels, twenty-five of which featured Colonel Charles Russell of the (fictional) British Security Executive. Haggard lacked Fleming's snooty dilettantism, and was better at creating subtle layers of political intrigue. As the series progressed he gained stature and popularity, and the books began to extend their range to include exotic locations and sexier set-ups.

For here was the problem: born in Croydon in 1907, Haggard, a former Indian civil servant and British establishment figure, was middle-aged by the time he started producing novels. His experience gave him an appealing air of cynicism and some strongly-held opinions about the British government, particularly in its strained relations with big business, but it also meant that he was heavily drawn to characters who spent their lives manoeuvring themselves around the political system. The public wanted Bond wandering into the Monte Carlo Casino with a fag on and a martini in his free hand. Gunplay and continental sex made for tartier adventures, but weren't really Haggard's field. His plots were first-rate, his world-weary characters were slyly intelligent and manipulative, but ultimately a great many scenes consisted of men arguing in offices.

In *The Unquiet Sleep*, a popular Valium-like drug is found to have devastatingly addictive qualities, and a parliamentary official is linked to its parent company. Colonel Russell finds each level of government involvement murkier than the next, in contrast to Fleming's approach, which leaves world domination to a few egotistical madmen. Haggard treats his women with more respect, too. Loyal wives and sensual lovers they may be, but they are also investigators and heroines with lives of their own. As for exoticism, try his character Miss Borrodaile, the elegant black-clad ex-French resistance fighter with a steel foot.

By the time Haggard wrote *The Power House*, his publishers had cottoned onto the Bond effect, and the paperback cover featured an alarming *décolletage* perched over a pile of roulette chips. His writing requires attention, but there are rewards for modern readers, especially in the sixties scenes that explore the sleazy private lives of civil servants. His books are out of print but not unavailable.

64. Dorothy Whipple

JB Priestley once described her as 'the Jane Austen of the twentieth century'. Dorothy Whipple (née Stirrup) was massively successful in her day, joining the ranks of Waugh and Greene with her second novel *Greenbanks*. Her popularity was no doubt helped by the grace and unostentatious simplicity of her prose, but – it's becoming a litany in this volume – she fell out of style after the war.

One of eight siblings, Whipple was born in 1893 just off the Edgware Road to a respectable family of manufacturers. She married a director of education 24 years her senior (a concern that wormed its way into her writing), and wrote *Young Anne*, the first of nine increasingly successful volumes. Her novels are nuanced tales in which families face social readjustment after becoming 'victims of the turbulence of the outside world'. Her characters discover that the tenacity of the spirit and the innate goodness of ordinary people help them to face life's shortcomings.

Two of her novels were made into British films: a family climbs the social ladder then faces disgrace in the noir-ish *They Knew Mr Knight*, while James Mason starred in *They Were Sisters*. The latter is a rather menacing tale of three siblings, their choices and the various levels of domestic abuse they suffer. Whipple's final novel, *Someone At A Distance*, concerns mid-life crisis and infidelity, and is considered by many to be her best. Whipple described it as 'a fairly ordinary tale about the destruction of a happy marriage.' If you want to see her style encapsulated, read its opening line.

Once again, Persephone Books did an excellent job of rescuing these lost books, which committed no greater sin than being unsensationally written (with hints of classic French writers) and beautifully constructed. There's no simple answer as to why Whipple fell quite so far from favour. Her characters are drawn from recognisable realities and prove highly capable of making their own decisions. It's not as though postwar female readers stopped believing in them. It was Whipple's curse to be writing about ordinary lives at a time when the world started to crave adventure. The everyday grind of managing at home during the war had radically transformed readers' appetites.

Is it possible to read books like these now and still find pleasure in them? Absolutely, because our emotional centres remain unchanged, so Whipple's novels and short stories are as valid as they ever were.

65. Peter Barnes

As the arteries of theatreland clog with clapped-out musicals, the authors of great plays are more in danger of being forgotten than most novelists. Plays become ephemeral if they fail to enter repertoires. The shock of their experience fades, and only the scripts remain. Peter Barnes is still often misunderstood by critics seeking easy tags. His work was elaborately constructed, intellectually rigorous and controversial, his language exact and demanding. It must also have been a bugger to memorise.

Barnes was born in Bow in 1931, but his parents moved to a geriatric coastal town to run an amusement arcade. Appropriately, his writing links death and jokes to create a dark carnival atmosphere. A part-time theologist, film critic and screenwriter, Barnes was one of the great proponents of anti-naturalism, a dazzling response to the dreary kitchen sink novels and plays of the fifties.

At a time when Monty Python was reconfiguring comedy, a number of authors including Peter Nichols, John Antrobus and Alan Bennett started incorporating Surrealism, disjunction and Pirandello-esque antics into their work. Barnes wrote *The Ruling Class*, a satire about power that nominally concerns a mad earl and his identification with Christ. Asked how he knows he's Jesus, his lordship replies, 'It's simple. When I pray to him I find I'm talking to myself.' A film version with Peter O'Toole was brave but problematic.

Barnes proved too uncomfortable for middle class audiences, never more so than in *Laughter!*, a horrifying but deeply moral comedy about office workers providing the paperwork for crematorium chimneys in Auschwitz, who are forced to realise their complicity.

Beloved by serious theatre actors like Guinness and Gielgud, Barnes later softened a little to write period comedies and monologues (perhaps because he became the father of triplets in his seventies), but not before turning out *Red Noses*, one of the few slapstick comedies set during the time of the Black Death. For this raucous tale of a troupe of performers touring afflicted French villages, he won a well-deserved Olivier award.

Barnes' screenplay for the film *Enchanted April* secured an Oscar nomination, and his history plays became more naturalistic, although he was always capable of dazzling *coups de théâtre*. Barnes wrote 'Write what you know is good advice for journalists. I write what I imagine, believe, fear, think.' To read his intense, rarely performed plays now is to see how far the theatre of ideas has lately fallen.

66. Matthew Phipps Shiel

HG Wells and MP Shiel were exact contemporaries, entering and leaving the world within a year of each other, but Wells' reputation as the father of science fiction has continued to grow, while Shiel has disappeared from bookshelves. Both were socialists with an interest in future fiction and scientific romances, and there is evidence that Wells was influenced by Shiel, but Shiel was a West Indies-born author writing in the flamboyant style of the decadent movement. Around the turn of the century he created the first future history series in science fiction with a trilogy that began with *The Last Miracle* (although more fairly, the books offer three unconnected alternative futures). This was followed by *The Lord Of The Sea*, based on a critique of the private ownership of land, but Shiel's reputation rests mainly on the third part of the sequence, *The Purple Cloud*. It's an apocalyptic novel that brushes off casual readers with a series of false starts, but settles down to become a truly extraordinary work of fiction.

The book was produced at a time when there was great interest in the unexplored Arctic, and tells the tale of a man named Adam Jeffson who travels there, only to return and find the earth decimated by a vast purple cyanide cloud. Without the constrictions of a moral society, crushed by the burden of terrible isolation, Adam wields a power that tips him from eccentricity into megalomania. Dressed as a sultan, he takes explosives from the Woolwich Arsenal and burns London down. Laying waste to cities becomes a habit, a cry of rage for his imprisonment on earth, and he destroys nations before meeting another survivor, a woman in Istanbul, who may have the key to his survival.

Shiel wrote twenty-five novels, but many are bland romances produced more for profit than the passion of language that shows in *The Purple Cloud*. Shiel's private life was, it seems, as decadent as his early writing. He served sixteen months' hard labour in prison for molesting his 12-year-old step-daughter, and showed a penchant for underage girls throughout his life and his fiction. He also reckoned himself the King of Redonda, a small inhospitable isle in the West Indies, but this may have been concocted as a joke at the expense of critics. His trilogy was published out of sequence, having first been serialised, and when I last looked, *The Purple Cloud* was available in a beautiful new edition.

67. Georgette Heyer

Georgette Heyer is not out entirely of print. A few of her books are readily available and regularly reprinted – but she has fallen into a strange and rather airless niche market, where once she was one of the most popular writers in the country. Heyer was a literary phenomenon who wrote bestsellers throughout her career without ever giving an interview or making any kind of public appearance. A recluse in her private life, she was driven to communicate with her readers through a series of light regency romances for which she had scant regard, saying only that 'I ought to be shot for writing such nonsense.'

Her novels received no critical acclaim, but sold so well that her name alone was enough to guarantee success. Fifty one novels, short story collections and mysteries were published, appearing at a rate of one or more a year throughout her life.

Heyer was born in London in 1902, and continued writing until her death in 1974. Her narratives were peppered with wicked dukes, hearty knights, feisty ladies and headstrong rakes whose amorous escapades unfurled against colourful historical backdrops. Along the way, horses rear, eyes flash, bosoms heave and ladies of quality exhibit a tendency to faint. Her pages are packed with arranged marriages, desperate elopements, crimes of passion and descriptions of the prevailing fashions. No wonder, then, that critics were sceptical and dismissed each arrival merely as 'the latest Georgette Heyer'. This gap between popularity and peer respect was created largely by Heyer's worldwide readers, who lapped up the romances while failing to notice their favourite author's meticulous attention to period detail.

Her books were a perfect combination of undemanding plot and colourful characterisation, but to my jaded eye at least, they seem almost parodic in their earnest desire to entertain. Most of the volumes stand alone, but four contain recurring characters. They're well-written, not very thought-provoking, but tremendously entertaining. And her work improved; her late comedies of manners now best stand the test of time.

Heyer left behind the unfinished manuscript of a serious mediaeval book, since published, that revealed her great skill and love of research. Although she left no early drafts, dismissed her first four novels and kept only one fan letter, she was greatly concerned that her books should provide historical accuracy. Why then was she so utterly self-deprecating about her work?

68. Robert van Gulik

At the start of the 20th century, authors like Sax Rohmer (real name: Arthur Ward) were penning tales of imperial adventurers battling 'yellow peril' conspirators, amidst a prevailing fear that the Chinese were inherently criminal by nature. Ward was attacked for his racial stereotyping at the time of publication, and now the novels are dismissed as absurd, colourful escapades reminiscent of the exploits of Indiana Jones.

Counterbalancing these stories were the erudite Judge Dee novels, created by Robert van Gulik. Born in 1910, van Gulik grew up in the Netherlands and Jakarta, before joining the foreign office to begin a lifetime of roaming the Far East. By the time he became the councillor of the Dutch embassy in Washington he was long established as an orientalist, a diplomat and expert player of the guqin, a delicate seven-string music instrument rather like a zither.

Although he also wrote essays and short stories, van Gulik remains best known for his excellent Chinese mysteries. These comprise some fourteen novels and short story volumes chronicling the career of a stern but fair-minded judge, based on a real-life 7th century Chinese detective called Di Renjie. Interestingly, the tales first found fame in oriental editions, before being translated into English in 1957.

The construction of the long novels is unusual. They take the form of several interwoven cases, and follow the traditional style (now itself forgotten) of Chinese detective stories. Despite the fact that he added elements from the much later Ming dynasty, van Gulik was greatly concerned with accuracy, and created a detailed career timeline for his main character, adding his own graceful illustrations and maps to help readers understand the judge's life.

As a magistrate, Dee was allowed up to four wives, so his personal life is complicated. What's more, several of the plot strands are based on real-life cases. Elaborate cruelties abound within them; there are headless corpses, lake phantoms, corrupted monks, nail murders, attacks by brigands, mysterious scrolls to be deciphered, but all these events are informed by the decency of the clear-eyed judge, whose understanding of human nature extends beyond thoughts of formal retribution.

Best of all, the stories feel authentic because they are filled with simple descriptions of Chinese life, the sights and sounds of a lost time lovingly recreated by a scholar who was immersed in the culture of the period. The books were acclaimed at the time of publication. The first Judge Dee novel, *The Chinese Maze Murders*, has since been republished, but the rest are harder to find.

69. Gavin Lyall

A bit of a man's man, was Gavin Tudor Lyall. In the 1960s he wrote tales of square-jawed men dodging bullets and doing man things, but his writing style was far from thick-ear. Married to the journalist Katharine Whitehorn (who has written lovingly about their marriage in her autobiography) Lyall's love of aircraft and all things mechanical provides the power for his early novels. Indeed, it's hard to think of his work without hearing the choking cough of a plane engine dying somewhere above hostile territory. Luckily, you only have to give his heroes a spanner to guarantee an escape attempt. The author was among the top British thriller-writers of the 1960s, and made his name with literate suspensers, most of them featuring butch chaps performing tough jobs in the changing political postwar climate.

His first big seller concerned dodgy pilots on *The Wrong Side Of The Sky*, and the paperback boasts an awesomely sexy sixties Pan cover. Researching meticulously, the writer built in a level of technical detail that instantly appealed to his male readership. Like Eric Ambler and Nevil Shute, there's something comfortingly solid about the Lyall style. His capable heroes travelled the world in beaten-up aircraft, trying to stay ahead of the law or the lawless. In 1965's award-winning *Midnight Plus One*, his pilot does a favour for an ex-Resistance comrade, protecting a businessman, but he's grounded and forced into a terrific extended cross-France chase. The film rights were purchased by Steve McQueen, but the star's death deprived us of the movie version.

Lyall suffered writer's block for five years, but returned with something new: a Le Carré-esque series of tough novels featuring Major Harry Maxim of the SAS. The BBC filmed the first, *The Secret Servant* with Charles Dance, but the writing was on the wall for spy fiction of this kind. Such derring-do could not survive the end of the Cold War. Lyall bounced back with another series, starting with *Spy's Honour*, set against the birth of the British Secret Service, just before the First World War. These were enjoyable romps in the style of John Buchan, but now played as retro adventures, and proved less popular.

Although his characters were pretty thinly defined, the pacey plots had the kind of clear through-lines rarely found in modern thrillers. Too much action is exhausting to read, but Lyall knew what to include and when to stop. Taken in the context of the times in which he wrote, they're still attractive additions to any library.

70. Maryann Forrest

Seeking out lost authors requires two kinds of detective work: I track them down, but if readers become interested, they have to locate their work. Throughout the process, one author continued to block further investigation. I knew the Australian-born Maryann Forrest was someone to check out when I read a description of her in *Time Out* as 'a stunning writer, so superb and alive a talent'. Then Anthony Burgess picked up on her first novel, describing it as 'deeply disturbing' but 'a keen literary pleasure'.

Here (Away From It All) was an adult *Lord Of The Flies* involving wealthy holidaymakers instead of schoolchildren. A Greek island has been ruined by opportunistic tourism; overrun with timeshares and package tours, its natives have been marginalised and employed as service personnel. One day an unspecified world event occurs which ends all contact with the island, so that foreign currency is suddenly rendered worthless. Hotel guests find themselves paying their bills with watches, rings and necklaces. But when the material goods run out, they need something else to barter with. And as the rules of civility become ever more strained, the islanders start to exact revenge.

The protagonist, a young mother, watches in horror as the unnamed island – the world in microcosm – breaks down into rebellion and anarchy. The revengers have Greek names but there is no racism here, because a silver thread of humanity runs through the characters, refusing easy demonization, and the heroine remains upbeat even as all hope fades.

The tale is post-apocalyptic and descends inexorably to a horrifying climax, but is written from a deeply personal viewpoint. Cormac McCarthy's *The Road* is probably the only book that comes close in its bleak subject matter.

Written in 1970, *Here* feels alarmingly prescient, but when I tried to find out more about its author I drew a total blank. One editor suggested that she had actually escaped the world by moving to the Greek island described in her novel, but this seemed unlikely as there were two other books, *Us Lot*, a dreamlike account of a young woman's drifting, hedonistic years and the darkly satiric *Immaculate Misconception*, written within three years of her first. It appears she was using a pseudonym, and although there were plenty of Mary Ann Forrests listed in the Australian electoral rolls, the trail ran cold after that. I decided to ask readers for help. All three books could still be found on the Internet, but there were no reprints and I was relying on those with long memories and bookshelves.

Some weeks later I received a letter which began: 'My first husband came across your piece about Maryann Forrest, asking if anyone knows where she is. Yes I know, for I am she. Come to lunch.'

I visited Polly Hope, polymath artist, sculptor and opera librettist, in London's Spitalfields, where she thrives in her graceful colour-filled studio house, along with any number of dogs, cats, chickens and friends, and found that she had adopted an alias (she had an Australian grandmother) to write the novel. Polly was living in Greece during the period of the military junta, and would very likely have faced deportation upon publication of the book. This raised an idea I hadn't considered: Perhaps other authors were also successful polymaths who simply sought to pursue varied careers. Polly covered her tracks so successfully that her three books remain tough to find. She remains one of the new friends I've made through this endeavour, and you'll find her again at the end of the book.

71. Robert Klane

So far, many of our neglected writers have been sensitive souls whose dazzling prose has fallen from fashion. Robert Klane is the opposite: loud, lewd, offensive and hilarious, his books kicked black comedy back into style with a mix of taboo-busting farce and broad Jewish schtick.

Born 1941, Klane has been described as 'Max Shulman spiked heavily with the Marquis de Sade', but also incited comparisons to Joseph Heller and JD Salinger. In his first novel, *The Horse Is Dead*, published in 1968, the hero Nemiroff works as a counsellor at Camp Winituck, which looks 'like a poorly run concentration camp'. Nemiroff's bullied childhood leaves him with a hatred of all children, and he soon declares war on his charges. By the time Parents' Day and the titular dead horse arrive, most barriers of good taste have fallen.

Klane's prose is as blunt as a chucked brick. He has no time for niceties, and recognises that the best dark comedy, like life, is painful, mean and short. *Where's Poppa?* (1970) may be the ultimate Jewish mother novel. Trapped at home with a senile parent, a dominated and sleep-deprived lawyer continually loses his cases and his girlfriends. His attempts to frighten his ancient mother to death must be nightly defeated by his guilt-laden brother, who runs a gauntlet of Central Park muggers in order to prevent matricide and halt the receipt of said mother into his own home. The film version, made with George Segal and Ruth Gordon, suffered a failure of nerve in the final furlong and avoided the novel's brilliantly ghastly Oedipal outcome.

Klane's third novel, *Fire Sale*, in which the owner of a

failing department store plans to have it torched for the insurance by hiring an arson-prone mental patient to do the job, was filmed with Alan Arkin and Sid Caesar. The books are oddly endearing because they capture the sheer unfairness of life, particularly as it was lived in the early 1970s. Like great farceurs before him, Klane tackled sex, family, madness and death, roughly in that order.

Klane eventually made the switch into film and television, writing several episodes of *M*A*S*H*, an unproduced sequel to *Grease* entitled *Greasier*, and making *Weekend At Bernie's, 1* and *2*, two mildly amusing films which, like Hitchcock's *Trouble With Harry*, featured a deceased leading character. His books are now all out of print, but worth picking up if you stumble across them.

72. Marjorie Bowen

An author whose life was as fascinating as her output, Marjorie Bowen was born Margaret Gabrielle Vere Campbell Long in 1885 on Hayling Island, Hampshire. Her mother had literary aspirations and her father was an alcoholic who died on the London streets. Long had no formal education, but used libraries and museums to provide herself with the tools she needed for a writing career. The family was poor and moved constantly to avoid clearing debts.

Bowen's first novel, *The Viper Of Milan*, set in 14th century Italy, was published to acclaim when she was just 21, but had first been rejected by eleven publishers who felt it was not the sort of thing a young Edwardian woman should write. Bowen received sixty pounds for her work, which she surrendered to the family, but her mother was jealous of her success and became increasingly embittered.

Margaret's money was banked in her ungrateful mother's name, and was spent as fast as she earned it. With each hard-won advance being frittered away on trivial luxuries and loans to her mother's hangers-on, Margaret seemed always panicked into writing for money, and never stopped being the family breadwinner. The discord affected her so badly that she wrote a brutally honest account of her life in *The Debate Continues*.

She entered her first loveless marriage with a demanding, sickly Sicilian in order to escape the cruelties of home, and eventually found happiness through her children. Despite the apparent wretchedness of her life, she wrote over 150 volumes under half a dozen pseudonyms, and tackled larger-than-life subjects in historical dramas, supernatural tales and mournful Gothic romances.

Critics have long considered her storytelling to be clear-eyed and efficient, her detail and description masterful, her understanding of human nature filled with compassion and sorrow. I could only locate a copy of *Dickon*, the story of Richard III, the last Plantagenet, written in a concise prose style which has somewhat fallen from fashion. Bowen illuminated a wide variety of passionate subjects by tackling them in novel form, and was widely admired by other authors, including Graham Greene. Would she be better remembered now if she had written at leisure, purely to indulge her obvious love of prose, instead of doing it to clear her mother's bills?

73. Bill Tidy

The case of Bill Tidy illustrates an unusual form of public amnesia. Daily pages of cartoons in the national press are common in US papers, which still run dated strips like *Blondie* (born 1930) and *Andy Capp* (born 1957) but the art of the British serial cartoon has died, and Bill Tidy represents a neglected peak of the form.

When *Punch* magazine folded after 150 years in 1992, a raft of familiar names vanished with it. In the UK a handful of artists, like the wonderful Surrealist John Glashan, also drew strips which evolved into long-running stories, but the most epic and peculiarly English exponent of these is Bill Tidy. His strip *The Cloggies* gently ribbed Northern customs through the adventures of a championship clog-dancing team, and ran in *Private Eye* for years. However, his magnum opus was *The Fosdyke Saga*, which appeared in the *Daily Mirror* and was eventually published in fourteen volumes, in a once-popular oblong paperback cartoon format which has now disappeared.

In a demented epic parodying Galsworthy and JB Priestley, the books chronicled the trials of a poor Lancashire family rising to the heights of wealth and fame through the late Victorian period into the early 20th century. The Fosdykes made their money by finding profitable new uses for tripe, and their adventures took them through every major national event, from Mafeking and Flanders to dogfights with the Red Baron, through peace rallies and zeppelins to the deck of the Titanic, and a valiant Lancastrian attempt on Everest by the Accrington Stanley Expedition. Along the way, all the major characters who caught the public attention made guest appearances, from Eliot Ness to the Loch Ness Monster.

Tidy wrote and drew all his marvellously energetic work, but what stands out is a strange mindset that avoids obvious jokes and goes for something which doesn't quite make sense while feeling entirely right. 'Stay,' begs an Arab sheik, clasping a portly harem girl, 'the night is young and you are enormous!'

Comedy doesn't always need explanation. It's about time, then, that a publisher packaged these lovely works into a single collection that could sit tidily on a shelf. At the time of writing, the author still surfaces with an occasional cartoon, and while his charmingly skewed humour is now probably a little outré for mass consumption, he happily continues to create his strange world, and will hopefully see the renaissance he deserves.

74. Shirley Jackson

If her name rings a bell, it might be because Shirley Jackson is finally receiving the critical attention she has so long deserved. Born in San Francisco in 1916, Jackson created a sensation by publishing a story in *The New Yorker* that generated a phenomenal amount of correspondence. Her brief tale, 'The Lottery', touched a nerve and demanded an explanation where none had been provided. It concerned a rural town in which a lottery takes place, but the winner of the lottery must face a horrifying sacrifice that's both biblical and incomprehensible. Having touched off a public furore, she nevertheless found an audience drawn to her style of calm, precise emotional detachment.

Jackson neatly tapped into the concerns of fifties America. 'It isn't fair, it isn't right' screams Mrs Hutchinson in 'The Lottery', and much of her short fiction deals with what was considered right at the time. The middle class was becoming more comfortable, but was also beset by fears of societal collapse. 'If people had been really honestly scared when you were young', says a character in 'The Intoxicated', 'we wouldn't be so badly off today.'

Jackson's novel *Lizzie* dealt with a woman suffering from multiple personality disorder. *The Haunting Of Hill House*, a novel regarded by many as one of the most powerful psychological ghost stories ever written, also explores female insecurities in greater depth than most novels of the period. 'No live organism', she writes, 'can continue for long to exist sanely under conditions of absolute reality.' And so the delicate Eleanor faces loneliness, madness, depression and imprisonment with a sense of inner stillness that ultimately turns her into a heroine.

To my mind, her best book was her last. *We Have Always Lived In The Castle* was chosen by *Time* magazine as one of the ten best novels of 1962. In it, two sisters and an ancient uncle huddle in psychotic solitude, and the girls create a set of rules for survival that make the hero of Iain Banks' *The Wasp Factory* seem entirely normal. Over the years I lost count of how many times this heartbreaking story was announced as a movie, but it remains unfilmed. Perhaps no-one will ever manage to recreate the twisted world that works so well on the page. It is perhaps the ultimate Goth novel, and is finally being marketed as such instead of being allowed to languish in obscurity.

Some thirty years after Jackson's early death at the age of 48, a box of previously unseen stories was found in a barn behind her house; they were published to great acclaim. It's sad that she did not consider them of sufficient quality to have them printed in her lifetime. In the US, the Shirley Jackson Awards have been established to acknowledge similar masters of the disturbing novel.

75. Dino Buzzati

It's surprising how many vanished authors have managed to survive in their short fiction rather than their novels, even though their full-length works received plaudits on publication. Dino Buzzati (1906-1972) is obscure even by bibliophiles' standards, so it's nice to be able to include him here, because he was an extraordinary writer.

A painter, poet, playwright, editor and journalist, Buzzati found fame with the publication of *The Tartar Steppe*, a disturbing novel reminiscent of Kafka and Camus, about a young soldier in a far outpost awaiting inundation by barbarians. The novel, which damns the military mindset, denies the reader the satisfaction of a final explanation, and in doing so captures the elusive contours of our real lives.

Buzzati completed five novels, comics, a number of plays and a still-popular children's book about bears in Sicily, but discerning editors can cherry-pick from his six volumes of powerful short stories, and one or two reprints have found their way into present-day English language collections. Buzzati's greatest strength lay here, in a kind of Italian magical realism that heightened the simple and practical with seemingly fantastic elements.

In 'Seven Floors', a businessman with a minor ailment is admitted to a hospital in which each floor denotes a different severity of illness, the ground level being reserved for those about to die. By accident, he soon finds himself being shunted down floor by floor…

In 'Just The Very Thing They Wanted', a touring couple visit a small town and find themselves denied the most basic human rights, the need to sit down, to drink, to rest, to gather their strength. Perhaps because translation forces his prose into a kind of universal English, his writing feels timeless. In 'The Elevator', from his collection *Restless Nights*, a lift takes its occupants on a journey far below the bottom of the building, but instead of producing a standard tale of the fantastic, Buzzati uses the situation to frighten his leading character into an honest declaration of love.

Buzzati's standing as a creative polymath probably set a time limit on his fame. How could you promote such a multi-talented writer overseas? Finding his work without paying a fortune for it is a labour of patience. A collection of stories was recently available on the Internet for around $250.

76. Oscar Wilde

Hang on. Hang on. Dear Oscar? Never off the London stage, Dame Judi, *a handbag*, that Oscar? There's another type of forgetfulness that occurs when we choose to remember authors by their most famous books or plays. Their lesser works get lost or sidelined. Few readers of *Oliver Twist* recall Dickens' round-robin collections like *Somebody's Luggage*. Tennessee Williams is treasured for *A Streetcar Named Desire* but not for 'The Mysteries Of The Joy Rio', one of around fifty exquisite short stories he penned. A good test of popularity is checking the number of reader reviews a book gets on Amazon. The average Harry Potter gets close to a thousand. For a long time, the collected fairytales of Oscar Wilde got just one. Although still technically available, they are rarely bought and read aloud anymore, as they were designed to be.

Even now, it seems there are readers who have issues with squaring the unrepentant 'somdomite' Wilde with these morally didactic stories, many containing overtly Christian messages. How do you deal with the repeated appearances of God?

'Bring me the two most precious things in the city', says God to one of his angels at the conclusion of *The Happy Prince*. The angel brings a leaden heart and a dead bird, a swallow who died in the service of a statue that gave away its finery (and heart) for a vain, unappreciative populace. Wilde uses God as a simple moral absolute, because it is needed in a story about degrees of selflessness and purity. Many of the tales are so heart-wrenchingly sad that they may now be too upsetting for tinies. Yet it sometimes seems as if the real Wilde resides here, rather than in his barbed, brittle plays. The Selfish Giant refuses to let others enjoy his garden, so everlasting winter invades it. The Nightingale pierces its heart with a thorn and bleeds upon The Rose, only for the gift to be dumped in a gutter, wasted by society. The Remarkable Rocket is a supercilious snob convinced of success, but instead suffers the humiliation of exploding unnoticed. The prescient tragedies of Wilde's life, if you seek them, are tucked into such forgotten corners.

77. Edmund Crispin

If you love an author, it's always a shame when you know you can pull their entire output from your bookcase with one hand. But to Robert Bruce Montgomery, born 1921, quality took precedence over quantity. Montgomery was the organist and choirmaster of St John's College, Oxford. This spirited, funny man turned to composing movie music and wrote six scores for the *Carry On* films. If you listen carefully to them, you'll spot musical allusions which are more amusing than anything in the scripts. He was also an important critic and editor, but best of all he wrote the Gervase Fen books, eleven dazzling, joyous volumes, all but one of which were produced between 1945 and 1951.

The first set the tone for what was to follow. Fen is Professor of English Language and Literature, and assumes that the reader can keep up with him as he spouts literary allusions while cracking crimes. The books are fast and fun, their hero charming, frivolous, brilliant and badly behaved. When investigating, Fen tends to dive into pubs, play word games or start singing badly, anything rather than stick to the job at hand. Sometimes he even breaks the fourth wall and makes jokes about his publisher.

In the first Fen story I read, the lanky don hijacks a philosophy lecture by noisily cracking walnuts and then loudly telling his own tale, which is far more interesting. In *The Moving Toyshop* Fen imagines titles for Crispin's novel while tied up in a cupboard. 'Fen steps in', said Fen. 'The Return of Fen. A Don Dares Death (A Gervase Fen Story). Murder Stalks The University. The Blood On The Mortarboard. Fen Strikes Back.' Then, to pass the time, he lists unreadable books, including 'Tristram Shandy' and 'The Golden Bowl'. The character becomes such a joy to be with that you usually don't care much about the crime, but the solutions are outrageously ingenious and highly implausible. The last book is weakest, written as Montgomery finally succumbed to drink; he was clearly having too much fun, but thankfully he put an awful lot of it on paper too. The problem now lies in tracking down all eleven volumes. Many are out of print, but some older copies are available second-hand from the US. Be warned: the covers are atrocious and bear no resemblance to the content.

78. Margery Sharp

Her best-known book was for children, and although Walt Disney bowdlerised it into animated tosh, it made Sharp more famous than she would otherwise have been. *The Rescuers* concerned a pair of rodent agents for the Prisoners' Aid Society Of Mice, sent on a mission that involves the daring rescue of a Norwegian poet and the thwarting of an evil Persian cat called Mamelouk.

Born Clara Margery Melita Sharp in Salisbury, 1905, her output included twenty-six novels for adults and fourteen stories for children. She often wrote from a male perspective and was entirely unsentimental, even when romantic moments were required. Her clear-eyed characters and fastidiously constructed, unpretentious plots made her work suitable for filming, so *Cluny Brown* and *The Nutmeg Tree* became movies, and she wrote *The Notorious Landlady* for Jack Lemmon and Kim Novak.

She was more interested in novels, though, and the craft of writing. 'I absolutely believe it is fatal ever to write below your best', she said, 'even if what you write may never be published.' She married a handsome aircraft engineer and lived happily ever after, but there were hints that she wanted her work to be taken more seriously, and that her comfortable life – the couple lived at the Albany, in Piccadilly – could have been more fulfilling. Virago, ever the rescuer of forgotten women authors, republished *The Eye Of Love*, one of her cleverest novels, a double-plotted gem that starts with a love affair between a parcel and a Spanish dancer (at a costume party). The rest of the adult books went out of print.

When accurately displayed, human emotions never

date; Sharp's novels, written across half a century, feel fresh despite the vernacular of the times. Her imagery is carefully chosen and always a delight. Describing a family of generous-natured women, she explains that they had reached 'a solar pitch of stately jollification', and so had Sharp's writing. She liked the words 'tureen' and 'vermin', the soft opening V of 'velvet', 'violets' and 'voluptuousness'. She cared deeply about words, which places her at odds with, and beyond the fashion of, the kind of women who now write pastel-cover tat for chicks and mummies.

79. Thomas Tryon

He had it all: charm, intelligence, style, popularity, success, and he was ridiculously handsome. Did I mention he was also dating a (male) porn star? Tryon played the lead in cult hit *I Married A Monster From Outer Space* and almost starred opposite Monroe in *Something's Got To Give*, until she was fired from the film. Bored with acting (and humiliated by Otto Preminger) he thought he'd write, and was damned good at that too. His novels included civil war sagas, and were popular successes. Three were filmed.

Tryon's style was American Expansive; grand themes and resonant plots, set in Connecticut or New England. His first novel, *The Other*, about a Russian grandmother teaching a dangerous game to two brothers, one gifted, one harmful, was reissued in a new edition with a contextualising foreword by Ramsey Campbell. The narrative contains a blindsiding mid-tale twist, and was subsequently filmed.

The next, *Harvest Home*, occupied *Wicker Man* territory. A family relocates to a perfect American town, but the idyllic setting proves deceptive. They have come here to enjoy the nation's old ways and get exactly what they wish for – at a price. Their dilemma is presented so appealingly that the reader cannot help but empathise, and is lured into the same nightmarish trap. A faithful but flat television version appeared with Bette Davis.

Tryon specialised in strong female characters, never more so than in *Lady*, a sweeping novel about the grand-dame who lightly rules her town between the wars, and who hides a lifelong secret that pinpoints America's damaging attitude toward miscegenation. Two portmanteau novels, interlinked tales concerning Hollywood players and their efforts to survive public taste and changing times, display insider's knowledge. One section of the first, *Fedora*, became the basis for a late Billy Wilder film.

By this time, though, something odd was happening to Tryon's writing. It had started to become twee and sugary in a way that seems to afflict certain types of popular American writing. By the time he introduced his hero as a white-faced mime in *Night Magic*, the books had become a trial to read. Tryon died tragically young, and his final works were published posthumously. He remains virtually unknown in the UK.

80. Dodie Smith

Dodie Smith has lately been rediscovered by a new generation of readers, but her curse was to have been eclipsed by Walt Disney, for Ms Smith wrote *The Hundred And One Dalmatians*, and it would be a shame if she was only remembered for the films. A Lancastrian born in 1896, Smith entered RADA but failed as an actress, and went to work for Heals furniture store. During this time she became a successful author, inspiring the headline 'Shopgirl writes play.'

After the success of *Dalmatians* she wrote the odd but delightful fantasy sequel *The Starlight Barking*, in which the dogs awake in a world where flying canines are running the country and all humans are asleep. Probably a step too far for Disney (especially as Cruella De Vil, the best villainess ever, only features in a slumbering cameo), the films returned to safer ground. Smith wrote four volumes of biography, nine novels and as many plays, including the charming *Dear Octopus*, but her crowning achievement began with the line: 'I write this sitting in the kitchen sink'.

I Capture The Castle appeared in 1948, and is both a parallel and the opposite of *Catcher In The Rye*, published three years later. It should surely be regarded as an equal, but whereas Holden Caulfield became an eternal symbol for rebellion, Cassandra Mortmain, Smith's teenaged heroine, was hampered by her background. She is, after all, a naive, optimistic bohemian trapped in her family's collapsing castle, in the middle of nowhere, while her beloved father – the one-time novelist who keeps the family in penury and isolation – struggles with his demons. The family – faded, vague stepmother and beautiful sister – are penniless, and the man they adore will drag them down into his own hell unless Cassandra can rescue him. Filmed on an overly tight budget in 2003, the film was a disappointment to lovers of the original. The last line of the book is 'Only the margin left to write on now. I love you, I love you, I love you.' What lies between those first and last lines deserves to be remembered.

81. Richard Bach

There are certain books only college students have the patience to read. In the seventies *Everything You Always Wanted To Know About Sex But Were Afraid To Ask* and *Zen And The Art Of Motorcycle Maintenance* were romping up the book charts in university towns. Each generation of wide-eyed freshers promotes one of these into the bestsellers, and at least it can be said that the standard is improving. For all I know, Jonathan Safran Foer's *Everything Is Illuminated* could be wonderful beyond page 17. Back in 1970, though, students were prepared to read a book exploring the life philosophy of a seagull.

Richard Bach's *Jonathan Livingstone Seagull* smashed the bestseller records. The slender square tome was to be found poking out of backpacks the world over. It concerns an anthropomorphic seagull that yearns to fly higher instead of just worrying about where its next whiting is coming from. Millions swallowed the inspirational Christian parable which, at 120 pages (heavily illustrated), took about twelve minutes to digest. It was so successful that it became a film consisting of shots of seagulls floating about to wiffly Neil Diamond songs, the overall effect of which was like lapsing into a coma caused by a getting a paper cut from a Hallmark card.

Bach followed this with *Illusions* and *One*, the message being that we transcend the gravity of our bodies and believe in ourselves, or something. Bach described *The Bridge Across Forever* as 'a story about a knight who was dying, and the princess who saved his life', which, as it concerned the second lady in his life, must have felt like a smack in the face to his first and third partners.

Claiming to be a direct descendent of Johann Sebastian Bach, the pilot-turned-novelist loved to explore the metaphysical aspects of flying. Bach's books are fictional versions of moments in his life that illustrate his philosophy. Call me a curmudgeon, but I like to think that his books fell from popularity because students became too sophisticated not to see through this kind of tendentious artery-hardening new age sputum.

(At the time of writing Richard Bach is in serious condition following a plane crash, we wish him well).

82. AP Herbert

Alan Patrick Herbert is almost out of print, and should have more readers. Herbert served in two world wars, survived Gallipoli, was a longstanding member of parliament and a social reformer who worked to end outdated divorce and obscenity laws, and was knighted by Churchill. He wrote the lyrics to popular songs and shows, and once highlighted the complexity of the British licensing laws by accusing the House of Commons of selling liquor without a licence. *Mr Gay's London* is his selection of crimes, court rulings and trials from the early 18th century, and is a lot more fun than it sounds. This interest in the absurdities of the legal system caused him to write the *Misleading Cases*, six volumes that operate on a wonderfully simple premise: a judge and a defendant square off against one another in a series of skirmishes designed to test the limits of the law.

Albert Haddock is a tireless everyman who would test the patience of a saint; he makes out a cheque on a cow and leads it to the office of the Collector of Taxes. 'Was the cow crossed?' 'No, your Worship, it was an open cow.' The question is, did he break the law? Haddock rows the wrong way up a flooded street, and is arrested. Haddock has his wineglass pinched by a waiter, and sues for damages. Haddock argues his way out of a charge of obstruction by referring to an obscure point in the Magna Carta. The cases were fictional, but were sometimes reported in the press as fact.

Along the way, big issues were aired and serious political points were scored. What is the meaning of education? What exactly are politicians? How much freedom do we really have? Herbert's tone is light, but the questions give one pause to think. *Misleading Cases* aired as a superb television series (now apparently lost) that ran for three seasons in the 1960s, with Roy Dotrice as Haddock and the wonderful Alastair Sim as the judge. Sim is exasperated but clearly an admirer of the defendant's knowledge of his rights. 'People must not do things for fun', Herbert warns. 'There is no reference to fun in any act of parliament.' Read Herbert and you bring back the fun.

83. Ronald Firbank

In a world that praises commonplace prose for its realism, it's nice to have Arthur Annesley Ronald Firbank, a sort of polar opposite to Andy McNab. Firbank, born 1886, had an eccentric narrative style that was an extension of his personality. For a man who wrote so much about society he was never comfortable in it, being too alcoholic, inarticulate and strange. Nevertheless, Firbank provides something of a natural link between Oscar Wilde and TS Eliot. He became a cult figure, which by his reckoning meant that he was read by a dozen clever people, but his work faded from even this attention.

His slim novels appeared in the aftermath of the First World War, but reflect nothing of the time. *The Flower Beneath The Foot* takes place in a vaguely Balkan state, and is as exotic as a poisonous orchid. His plots are dismissible, but the dialogue is a distilled essence of the epigrammatic. 'Whenever I go out', the king complains, 'I get the impression of raised hats.' 'Raised hats?' 'Nude heads, doctor.' This deeply shy, whispily neurasthenic author is important for a singularity of vision that proved inspirational. Joe Orton certainly absorbed his peculiar speech rhythms, recognising a truth in Firbank's dialogue: conversation need not sound real to have veracity.

His prose condensed whole worlds while leaving much unsaid, in a way that is finally almost fashionable. Asked for his opinion of literature, he admitted that he adored italics; a typically oblique Firbankian remark. His books contain party chatter consisting of disconnected words and phrases, much as we might actually perceive them. Infamously, one chapter comprised nothing but eight identical exclamations of the word 'Mabel!' Dilettantes drift dreamlike through his pages, tainting the aesthetic style that Wilde venerated. Firbank could not write or live in any other way. His novels were scribbled on postcards in hotel rooms heavy with flowers, but at a dinner party given in his honour, he consumed a single pea.

Being shallow is exhausting work, and can make exhausting reading, but Firbank is an example of a timeless author who should not be forgotten, because he is utterly unique.

84. Gladys Mitchell

Born in 1901, she was one of the 'Big Three' female mystery novelists, judged the equal of Dorothy L Sayers and Agatha Christie, but that's not quite accurate – she's more like a mad combination of both. Philip Larkin loved her and many admired her mordant and morbid mysteries. Diana Rigg starred in some bland TV versions of her novels that turn her Mrs Bradley character into a glamorous Miss Marple. The exposure has resulted in new demand for her books, which is good because they're more interesting than Christie's, if more problematic. Virago republished *The Rising Of The Moon*, but there are some sixty-six other volumes, a few of which have lately started reappearing.

Mitchell's old lady detective has little of Miss Marple's cosiness. She's physically repulsive, parchment-skinned and usually likened to a vulture or even a pterodactyl, thrice married and witch-like. In *Dead Men's Morris* she's described as having 'the maternal anxiety of a boa-constrictor which watches its young attempting to devour their first donkey'.

Mitchell was a schoolteacher who believed in the idea of the professional, progressive and somewhat Sapphic woman. Her title character was controversial and emancipated, and even considered murder justifiable if the occasion demanded. With such an outspoken heroine, Mitchell naturally made enemies. *The Spectator* described her as 'a tiresome old trout' whose mannerisms were the most trying in detective fiction, but many adored her work. Her murder cases have ambiguous solutions, and an air of the supernatural is never entirely banished from them. Her plots are on the farthest side of credulity, but to worry about realism is to miss the fun of her storytelling.

In *Merlin's Furlong* a necromantic don runs a coven of witches. In *The Mystery Of A Butcher's Shop* the victim is minced into sausages and hung from hooks. Ultimately, Christie remained safer and more controlled, while the wild-eyed complexity of Mitchell's uber-eccentric mysteries got the better of her. She tested the constraints of the murder genre by pushing them to breaking point, and by surprising too much she often disappointed – therein lies the clue to her canonical absence. But a flawed gem can still sparkle.

85. T Lobsang Rampa

WH Auden was wrong: there are some books which are best forgotten. By the time the memoir of a Tibetan monk entitled *The Third Eye* turned up on the desk of Secker & Warburg, it had been turned down by most leading houses. S&W took a punt and published it in 1956, and the book shot into the bestseller lists, with the esteemed *Times Literary Supplement* suggesting it was close to being a work of art. Doubts were quickly raised by Tibetan scholars; after all, the book included trepanation as a standard procedure for induction into priesthood, neophyte monks zipping about on giant kites, and Rampa's meetings with both his mummified former incarnation and an abominable snowman.

The press scented a story and exposed Rampa as a Devon plumber called Cyril Hoskin, who had never been near Tibet. This Blavatskyan revelation did not appear to bother his readers, who were happy to purchase another eighteen volumes of his Tibetan memoirs. Hoskin held back a late chapter involving his visit to the planet Venus, and said he had been possessed by the spirit of the monk after falling out of a tree while trying to photograph an owl. He further stated that his book *Living With The Lama* had been dictated by his Siamese cat Mrs Fifi Greywhiskers. Naturally this was enough to convince his credulous new age followers. With an entire industry springing up around him, as well as his family turning out books to capitalise on his success, Rampa grew weary of being described as a con-man and decamped to Canada, where he remained until his death in 1981. By now he had many new Canadian fans who accepted the books as proof of Buddhist principles, and were happy to endorse his unpublished chapters on flying saucers. They still maintain his fan site, should you wish to purchase the latest Lobsang Rampa calendar.

For non-believers the books are problematic, especially when Hoskin explains auras or soul transference in terms that would make any scientist fall off a chair laughing. Still, the books give an alarming insight into the naivety of ideas about exoticism in the postwar spiritual vacuum of the 1950s, and will always be tracked down by intellectually inert seekers of easy enlightenment. And, apparently, a handful of Canadians.

86. William Sansom

Here's a truly forgotten author, all but expunged from literary history. William Sansom was once described as London's closest equivalent to Franz Kafka. He wrote in hallucinatory detail, bringing every image into pin-sharp focus. It was his strength and weakness; it made his stories hauntingly memorable, but his technique often left his characters feeling under-developed. His style was as cool and painstaking as that of Henry Green, also a wartime firefighter. His collection *Fireman Flower, and Other Short Stories* may be his pinnacle. In 'The Little Room', a nun waits for death after being bricked up in her windowless cell for an unnamed transgression. To make her fate worse, a meter on the wall marks the incremental loss of the air in the room, and Sansom describes her changing state of mind with clinical precision and a certain passion.

'The Equilibriad' owes a little too much to Kafka but shares the same strangeness, as the hero awakes to find himself only able to walk at a 45 degree angle. He was good with an opening hook; one story starts 'How did the three boys ever come to spend their lives in the water-main junction?' Sansom's publisher described his work as 'modern fables', but what makes them so ripe for rediscovery is their freshness and currency. His characters face inscrutable futures with patience and resignation, knowing that they can do little to influence the outcome of their lives. Sometimes terrible events, like the collapse of a burning wall, slow down and expand to engulf the reader.

One of his strangest tales is 'The Long Sheet', in which captives are required to wring out a great wet sheet with their hands, and the process is described in flesh-smarting detail. Nor can the sheet ever be completely dried, because fresh moisture is constantly sprayed on it. But the final lines of the story reveal the true nature of torment while pointing the way to another prescient writer, JG Ballard. Sansom writes of head-aching hatreds and hopeless ecstasies, of malevolent objects and wasted lives. In his short fiction, he'd describe a taxi or an umbrella in a way that eluded him with the characters of his novels. He fell from favour, but now there is a movement to rediscover his finest works.

87. Peter Tinniswood

In my doomed quest to rehabilitate popular writers whose fame has been diminished by time and fashion, no-one is more deserving than Peter Tinniswood. There's a strong tradition of Northern comic writers who can hold tragedy and comedy in harmonious balance. Keith Waterhouse, Alan Sillitoe and David Nobbs also spring to mind.

Nobbs and Tinniswood were scripting partners, but went separate ways in their literary styles. Nobbs wrote the Reginald Perrin books, while Tinniswood commenced the long-running saga of the Brandon family with *A Touch Of Daniel*, which was popular enough to be serialised by the BBC. He's a lovely scene-setter: 'It was the time of year when bus conductors first appear in linen jackets.' His deadpan throwaway style translated poorly to television.

He wrote the surreal and much-loved cricketing series *Tales From The Long Room*, but was capable of stranger stories. When an author is made more popular by television adaptation, the success seems to remove longevity from his unadapted work. I can think of no other reason why his comic masterpiece has disappeared from the public radar.

The Stirk of Stirk is a highly peculiar prose poem that drops the reader into Robin Hood's darkest winter as, with rumbling stomach and perishing soul, the bandit faces his greatest enemy. Hood knows that creeping age and his inability to live up to his own legend will finish him off, yet simply refuses to die. The book is suffused with Northern chill and melancholy, but even in the blackest moments Tinniswood lights candles of hope. Here a laugh is described as 'a sound that would curdle the eggs in a goldcrest's womb' and 'saliva makes bitter fountains in the mouth' as the starving Hood staggers on into history – and out of the bestsellers' list.

This kind of heightened stylisation has fallen from popularity. Reading Tinniswood is like skimming any recent book on fast-forward, such is his ability to drag the reader through a colourful story. At his best, he's capable of reminding you that reading should always be a pleasure, never a chore. *A Touch Of Daniel* was reissued in 2001, two years before he died.

88. Victoria Holt

Stay with me – this gets complicated. Victoria Holt's real name was Eleanor Hibbert (née Burford), born in Kensington, 1906. After signing books as Elbur Ford (a contraction of her birth-name), she used pseudonyms including Jean Plaidy (a name taken from a Cornish beach), Philippa Carr, Kathleen Kellow and others, and wrote around 200 historical novels. She sold staggering amounts, in the region of 100 million copies. Lately, there have been some excellent reissues, so it's a good time to rediscover Britain's most popular historical novelist. She was feted for blending accurate period detail with strong plots and rich characterisation, so what happened to 'The Queen of Romantic Suspense'?

Burford was first published in 1941 for an advance of £30. Soon she was writing about Catherine De Medici, Charles II, Katherine of Aragon, Marie Antoinette and Lucrezia Borgia. Her style had enough gusto to draw polite applause from the critics, but her public adored her. This wasn't enough; she chronicled criminal cases, then embarked upon great cycles of novels in chronological order, covering the Normans, Plantagenets, Tudors, Stuarts, Georgians and Victorians. She branched into Gothic romance, mystery, non-fiction and children's books, and particularly enjoyed portraying feisty women of independence and integrity who fought for liberation.

Her viewpoints ring true: Hitler, she says in *The English Are Like That*, made the fatal mistake of frightening the English. Hamlet, she notes, is not incapable of action; he kills his man three times in the play. It's hard to find anyone with anything bad to say about her ideas, which makes her disappearance even stranger.

Perhaps her ubiquity rendered her disposable; popularity rarely guarantees posterity. Then there were those horrible pastel covers that reminded one of Quality Street chocolates. The truth is that popular historical fiction for women became unfashionable, just as surely as men stopped reading tales of kings and explorers. In came chick-lit and laddish stories that eschewed any mention of our collective history. Hibbert died on a cruise between Greece and Egypt, in her eighties. 'Never regret', she once said. 'If it's good, it's wonderful. If it's bad, it's experience.'

89. R Austin Freeman

Beware the author who follows in the wake of a bestselling series, for he will surely be forgotten. Sherlock Holmes spawned many imitators, including R Austin Freeman's charming mysteries, set in the Edwardian era. Dr Thorndyke is a barrister and man of medicine who, armed with his little green case of detection aids, sets out to solve puzzles that would scarcely interest today's police: a collapsed man who later vanishes, an ingeniously forged fingerprint, a crime scene more interesting than the act that occurred there.

His books began as homages (Thorndyke has his own Watson, named Jervis) but quickly developed their own style. Freeman was a doctor, and used his training more believably than Conan Doyle. He understood the tangled workings of the courts and advances in science such as the forensic power of X-rays, and incorporated them.

In *The Eye Of Osiris*, an Egyptologist vanishes from a watched room and must be presumed dead in order for his will to reach probate – but the will in question has a bizarre clause which makes it impossible to honour. Like WS Gilbert before him, Freeman takes great delight in outlining the peculiar properties of paradox. 'A man cannot deposit his own remains', cries Thorndyke in exasperation, as he deals with recalcitrant jurors, bovine policemen and potty witnesses.

Freeman also invented the opposite of the whodunnit, the 'inverted mystery', the how-will-he-be-caught? puzzle. If Dr Thorndyke lacks Holmes' sense of mystery he's more thorough when it comes to technical detail – 'The Man

With The Nailed Shoes' hinges entirely on a study of footprints and *The Eye Of Osiris* has a lengthy examination of embalming processes. His dialogue exchanges are also more freewheeling and sarcastic. 'I am a confounded fool!' says a character, as the reason for a corpse's finger being severed dawns on him. 'Oh, don't say that', says Jervis. 'Give your friends a chance.'

Freeman treats criminals in a more balanced manner than Conan Doyle. His working class characters – particularly in *Mr Polton Explains* – are decent, skilled and hard-working, but are still crushed by the system. His thirty-odd books are certainly worth rediscovery.

90. Lady Cynthia Asquith

Female authors seem to excel at cruel stories with emotional and possibly supernatural tints, using apparitions, fears and forebodings to indicate heightened states of unspoken emotional distress. In Charlotte Perkins Gilman's 'The Yellow Wallpaper' (now a staple on every English student's comparative literature list), a wife possibly suffering from post-natal depression descends into madness after being quarantined by her husband and doctor, with nothing to do except stare at the increasingly disturbing patterns in her bedroom wallpaper. The story was used by a generation of feminists to condemn marital inequalities, and is regarded as a classic. But there are many whose names have lapsed from familiarity.

Lady Cynthia Asquith was the daughter-in-law of the Prime Minister Herbert Asquith, and belonged to the literary aristocracy. As well as writing novels and ghost stories, she was an important anthologist and the editor of a series of popular collections. A friend to both DH Lawrence and LP Hartley, she spent two decades working for JM Barrie. She used her powerful literary connections to persuade an astonishing array of big names into her anthologies, many of which have never been bettered.

Asquith was a storyteller in her own right, and produced a series of fantasies with the ring of truth, collected in a number of volumes, the best being *This Mortal Coil*, nine tales of spectral vengeance and unease in high Victorian style. Her stories conjure up a world of things unnamed and half in shadow, where the past is never far from the present. Typically, in 'The Playfellow', a lonely child adopts a malevolent invisible companion who may be more real than anyone imagines. As the 20th century progressed and private subjects could be dissected on daytime TV shows, there was suddenly no need for this kind of soft-spoken fiction, where the cruelties of men were visited on women in such a stealthy, unwholesome fashion that heroines were often driven mad. Mental instability and hysteria are seen as signs of weakness, and our female characters are stronger now. Paradoxically, Asquith is best remembered for her non-fiction works on the female members of the royal family, strong women almost to a fault.

91. Peter Van Greenaway

No, not the one who directed *The Draughtsman's Contract.* This author was a lawyer-turned-novelist who wrote topical, political, satirical thrillers. At his best he combined popular fiction with a rare passion and erudition. *The Destiny Man* concerns a ham actor who seizes a last chance for stage fame when he discovers a missing Shakespeare folio on a train. There is a crime involved, but the novel's impetus derives from seeing if the hero – who has wangled sole rights to the play's performance – can redeem himself by rising to the role's challenge. Van Greenaway even has the nerve to create chunks of the bard's missing play from scratch, and pulls them off with panache.

Terrorism was a recurring theme in his prescient political thrillers. *Take The War To Washington* involved a group of Vietnam veterans who crash a passenger airliner into the Pentagon and launch a series of terrorist attacks on tall buildings in the US, in order to wreck the nation's international status, ending its financial dominance. *The Man Who Held The Queen To Ransom And Sent Parliament Packing*, published in 1968, describes a very British Victorian coup, played lightly for laughs, while scoring some nice points about British statesmanship.

Van Greenaway was popular enough to see his books packaged as mass-market paperbacks, and his suspenser *The Medusa Touch* was filmed with Richard Burton. The book further developed his interest in individuals taking control of their lives by any means necessary, but this time he added a paranormal aspect that reflected the righteous anger of the seventies. Burton played a disturbed author with a 'gift for disaster' who survives a violent attack by an unknown assailant. While he hovers in a state between life and death, flashbacks reveal that he can influence events and remove people who stand in his way with the power of thought. Van Greenaway turns his hero's ability to cause telekinetic catastrophes into a powerful moral tool that reflects the anti-establishment mood of the times. The author's peculiar talents were suited to the period in which he wrote but somehow transcended them, so that the books are still intriguing.

92. Patricia Carlon

When it came to putting women in dangerous situations and wringing suspense from them, Carlon was up there with another Patricia, Highsmith. Born in 1927 in Wagga Wagga, New South Wales, she wrote nerve-wracking novels with strong Australian themes, but was unable to find a publisher for them locally.

In the UK, Hodder & Stoughton picked up her best work – she produced fouteen novels between 1961 and 1970, starting with *Circle Of Fear* – and published them to acclaim. An American publisher discovered her novels by chance in a London bookshop, and an Australian did the same in New York, so her books were eventually picked up for publication in her native country forty years after she had become a success in Britain. Her writing was intelligent, hard-hitting and unsentimental, her prose deceptively simple (as was the style of suspense writing then), but there was something odd about it…

The Whispering Wall is fairly typical of her work. In it the elderly heroine, Sarah, is confined to her bed by a stroke while a sinister group of individuals plots against her. They assume that because she can't communicate she doesn't understand, but she is only too aware of their intentions and is determined to foil their plans. Her only ally is a girl traumatised by rape. The narrative has an atmosphere of claustrophobic menace, and is excruciatingly intense. In *Hush, It's A Game*, a little girl is locked in a kitchen by her babysitter, who is murdered. Then the murderer realises that there's someone else in the apartment…

This ability to sustain tension to an unbearable degree would have made her perfect for adaptation by Alfred

Hitchcock, who came to the rescue of so many of these authors, but Carlon was in the wrong time and place. She never married and lived alone, right next door to her parents in suburban Sydney. She only communicated with her publishers by letter. By this time her agent had noticed an obvious theme running through her books – all of her heroines experience a strong sense of isolation.

A little more research revealed the reason. Carlon had been deaf since the age of eleven, and understood what it was like to feel lonely and unable to communicate to others, so she recreated the sensation in her books, producing variations on a theme that never actually included deafness.

She eventually received the recognition she deserved in her homeland, and Soho Press republished her books in the UK.

93. Edgar Wallace

Conceived in a cupboard, born in Greenwich in 1875, and raised through a complex set of circumstances in a theatrical troupe by his mother, Wallace ended up selling newspapers in Ludgate Circus at the age of eleven, but he was to become one of the most ubiquitous authors of the early 20th century. Now he has a society with members in over twenty countries, and – an ultimate British accolade – there's a pub named after him off Fleet Street. But although he has hardly ever been out of print, how many people have read Edgar Wallace?

His first novel *The Four Just Men* was a prototype of the modern thriller, and concerned four handsome young vigilantes who kill in the name of justice. Ambitious and attuned to the power of marketing, the often childishly naïve writer launched a 'guess the murder method' competition that went horribly wrong after dozens submitted the correct answer, expecting to be paid in full. After causing two further law suits to befall the *Daily Mail*, he was fired from his job and started the 'Sanders Of The River' stories, which are steeped in the colonial attitudes of the times and rarely reprinted. They were, however, made into a film starring the excellent Paul Robeson.

Only months after his beloved wife died, Wallace became rich and famous. The success of a crime novel called *The Ringer* led to an extraordinary deal. He gave the film company British Lion a first option on all his future output. Despite suffering from undiagnosed diabetes, his energy was prodigious. He ventured into politics, then headed for Hollywood. In 1931 he began the five-week writing stint that resulted in *King Kong*. In this draft it was established that the ape was thirty feet tall, and was killed by a bolt of lightning hitting the Empire State Building. Wallace sadly died before seeing the completed film.

A famously fast writer, it was a standing joke that if someone telephoned Wallace and was told he was writing a book, they'd reply 'I'll wait.' He produced around 175 novels, twety-four plays, hundreds of articles and short stories, and about 160 films have been made from his work, including *The Edgar Wallace Mysteries*. I count twelve novels written in 1929 alone, but popularity does not always translate to longevity, and Wallace's slam-bang tales are often regarded as unsubtle and improbable. It was said that the King of Thrillers' heart was left behind in Fleet Street.

94. Roland Camberton

In the 1950s there was a minor fashion for proletarian literature, the dissection of the gutter-life of Londoners, cataloguing the conversations of scroungers, drunks and mugs as they burrowed between tobacco-tinged pubs and shabby rented rooms. Their typical chronicler would be a condescending dilettante hankering for a bit of rough.

Not so Camberton, whose *nom de plume* was a combination of Camberwell and Brixton, real name Henry Cohen. He rose from an orthodox East End Jewish background to become a teacher, copywriter, translator and novelist, and wrote three picaresque novels, although one of those, *Tango* about a hitch-hiking trip around Britain, was rejected by his publisher. He died at the age of 44, but the two books he managed to publish, *Scamp* and *Rain On The Pavements*, have rightly inspired admiration.

Scamp was published in 1950 and won the Somerset Maugham Award, but it had been the subject of critical opprobrium, perhaps because it didn't have much of a plot beyond outlining the rise and fall of the titular Bloomsbury literary review created by a scruffy pseudo-intellectual. *The Times* suggested that he was devoid of any literary gift, but Camberton's style had come too early, before the fashion for realism that was branded 'kitchen sink'. He was an outsider even among other Jewish outsider writers, so secretive that he was rumoured to be gay, but this proved not to be the case.

His second book was primarily a stitched-together collection of anecdotes about his Jewish childhood in Hackney, but after he failed to sell the third he simply vanished. Had he not done so and persevered, he might have caught the right time for his writing and become a public success.

But others were gathering together scraps of his past, including the writer Iain Sinclair and the author's own daughter, who shared details of Camberton's affair with her mother. Slowly the picture emerged of a man who may have changed his identity because of anti-semitic fears and the desire to assimilate and adopt a better life.

Sinclair's most dramatic find was discovering the existence of a tape which William Burroughs and a mutual friend had drunkenly recorded with Camberton, and although many details were now filled in, much still remains missing. One of his fictional characters was a failed writer who shunned the world of literature – a role Camberton himself chose. His books were finally republished by New London Editions.

95. Elizabeth Taylor

It must have been odd for a novelist with such a horror of publicity to have to share her name with an opposite. Taylor felt that her life was not worth bothering readers with. 'The whole point is that writing has a pattern and life hasn't. Life is so untidy. Art is so short and life so long. It is not possible to have perfection in life but it is possible to have perfection in a novel.'

She came from a quiet, bookish, middle-class family in Reading, was a lifelong Labour supporter and married the owner of a confectionary company. Her uneventful world provided her with the research for novels and short stories about everyday life, but what effortless novels they seem, filled with acute grace notes.

At Mrs Lippincote's was a sensitive portrait of an officer's wife, and must have touched many at the time of its publication, 1945. It was followed by eleven more novels, including *Palladian*, which reads like latter-day Charlotte Brontë. This most English of writers had the ability to create richly populated worlds. Her plots involve artists and their exploiters, affairs and marriages, small betrayals, intellectual alliances, respectability and disappointment, and fall so naturally into place that they don't feel plotted at all. Of course they are, and this is their beauty, but it has taken a long time for this style of low-key writing to come back into fashion, and Taylor's books are once more appearing on shelves. They're a testament of quality to a woman whose life was considered so devoid of incident that her friend Elizabeth Jane Howard turned down a request to write her biography. Ivy Compton-Burnett described her as looking like someone who had never had to wash her own gloves.

But there may have been more to Taylor than met the eye. Her letters were mostly burnt, and revelations have been hinted at. Certainly, beneath the polished exterior of her prose there's a surprising amount of violence and tragedy. An early taste for melodrama included accidents, suicides and glimpses of sexual cruelty. It wasn't all birdsong and flower-arranging.

Her most peculiar and ambiguous book is *The Real Life of Angel Deverell*, about an Edwardian lady novelist who becomes a huge success. The joke is that, although sincere, she's a truly appalling writer, and there's a suggestion that Angel is Taylor's alter-ego. *Angel* was filmed by Francois Ozon in 2007.

96. Gerald Kersh

These days London's Soho streets are not so mean. The undercurrent of corruption is still there, but now it involves property speculators, not spivs and bookies. Once, though, London low-life writing involved getting in with the wrong people, rather than just hanging out in media clubs. Kersh, born 1911, was the real deal, a bodyguard, all-in-wrestler and cinema manager for whom fighting and rough-sleeping were a way of life, and writing was as necessary as breathing.

His first novel, the thinly veiled autobiography *Jews Without Jehovah*, upset several members of his family so much that they filed libel suits against him.

The hero of *Night And The City* is a tough-talking Soho loser who fancies himself an American gangster. Unlikeable and self-deceiving, he fails to improve himself, although the book has a strong moral viewpoint. There were two film versions, one with Richard Widmark, the other with Robert De Niro. Both fall far short of the original.

Kersh was buried by a bomb in World War Two but bounced back as a quicksilver talent, writing short stories for *The Evening News* one day, producing character sketches, columns, articles and radio scripts the next. His wonderful short stories – which included a tale about a pilot who ages backwards and the Mona Lisa smiling to hide her bad teeth – were sometimes accepted as factually accurate. In these tales, which embraced every possible genre, resided his fame – but he should really have been lauded for *Fowlers End*, about a venal, hilariously Falstaffian cinema owner. Most critics ignored this masterpiece, although the ever-perceptive Anthony Burgess pronounced it one of the century's finest comic novels.

Kersh's other great novel is *The Thousand Deaths Of Mr Small*, about a man held back by all that he learned as a child. One by one, Mr Small's hopes of achievement are removed until he is left immobile. Kersh himself achieved a lot, but his rambunctious life, punishing working hours and natural *nostalgie de la boue* usually left him on the run from creditors or in hospital.

When he died in 1968, Kersh left behind stories and novels filled with a dazzling gallery of criminals and artists, characters filled with love and loathing, and carrying the seeds of their own destruction. It's a mystery as to why he is not regarded as a great British writer of the 20th century. The good news is that London Books republished his best works.

97. Michael Gilbert

'Watch his career', said his publisher. 'With *Close Quarters* you are in on the beginning.' Hodder & Stoughton's prophecy proved far-sighted, for their new author went on steadily producing for the next six decades. *Close Quarters* was the most English of mysteries, one concerning cathedrals and crosswords, layered with the kind of twinkling charm you find in the work of Edmund Crispin and other postwar mystery authors.

With a poet father and a novelist mother it was not surprising Gilbert chose to write, but his interest in crime spread to both sides of his career; he tackled his first mystery while studying for a law degree. But it was 1939, and an eventful war put his plans on hold. He became a prisoner of war in Italy, escaping during the Italian surrender and later using the experience of being a PoW and walking to freedom in *Death In Captivity* and *The Long Journey Home.*

Gilbert wrote during his train trips up from Kent to Lincoln's Inn Fields each morning, eventually producing 30 novels, four plays and hundreds of short fictions. During the war he had continued studying by riding around the Circle Line tube and using their electricity rather than his own. It was typical of his ingenuity, and he applied this talent to a series of whodunits that won him acclaim, the most devious being *Smallbone Deceased*, in which the mummified victim is found in a deed-box.

Postwar Britain was filled with the kind of bureaucratic officials Gilbert found annoying, and he took revenge on them in his books while recreating his legal mentors as fictional heroes. Although Gilbert's novels conform to the American description of 'Cosies' insofar as they feature

English institutions and rituals, there's a darker seam in his later tales that surfaces most powerfully in *The Night of the Twelfth*, which concerns the murder of children and contains echoes of the Moors Murders. He used his experience in law to flavour and inform his novels (he was solicitor to the alcoholic and awkward Raymond Chandler), and although I find his spy stories impenetrable, others better qualified reckon them highly.

Surprisingly, his quality did not diminish with age, and he wrote one of his finest courtroom dramas, *The Queen Against Karl Mullen*, at the age of eighty. Another surprise: he's making a bit of a comeback, and a few of his books can once more be found as reprints.

98. SS Van Dine

Raymond Chandler described him as 'probably the most asinine character in detective fiction', but upper class amateur sleuth Philo Vance was a hugely popular character in the 1920s, in books, films and on radio. Vance was the creation of SS Van Dine, the pseudonym of Willard Huntingdon Wright (1888-1939), a liberal US writer and art critic who authored *What Nietzsche Taught* and *Misinforming The Nation*, a vitriolic anti-British rant against the *Encyclopædia Britannica.*

Unfortunately, his plans for a lofty literary career were derailed by cocaine addiction. His doctor's solution was to confine him to bed for two years. Bored, he turned to reading detective stories and realised he might be able to make money. Adopting a pen name, he wrote *The Benson Murder Case* and seven more in the series, the early ones making him rich. As a dilettante and a poseur, he revelled in the high life but regretted losing his highbrow status.

With an expensive lifestyle to support it made more sense to write murder mysteries, and his vast knowledge of them led him to create a celebrated article entitled 'Twenty Rules For Writing Detective Stories'. The rules are still followed today. No.5 states: 'The culprit must be determined by logical deductions – not by accident or coincidence or unmotivated confession. To solve a criminal problem in this latter fashion is like sending the reader on a deliberate wild-goose chase, and then telling him, after he has failed, that you had the object of his search up your sleeve all the time. Such an author is no better than a practical joker.' Some of the rules, such as No.3's 'There must be no love interest', have now been superseded.

However, Wright didn't always stick to his own rulebook and is sometimes accused of cheating. He was very good at characterisation, but his frequently implausible plots didn't necessarily contain clues that would allow the reader to work out the solution. Even so, they were a lot of fun to read.

Wright's mysteries fell from fashion, but by now he was writing short films for Warner Brothers. At the time of his death he had flopped with an unpopular experimental novel that blurred fact and fiction called *The Gracie Allen Murder Case*, and had written another for the glamour-skater Sonja Henie, which was published after his death as *The Winter Murder Case*. His novels are all out of print, but can now be found in electronic formats.

99. Robert Aickman

Richard Marsh, the Victorian author of *The Beetle,* who will provide our 100th author, had a grandson who became regarded by many as the finest exponent of the modern ghost story. Although Robert Fordyce Aickman (born 1914) trained to follow in the footsteps of his architect father, he first became a conservationist, and is best remembered for co-founding the Inland Waterways Association, set up to restore and preserve the English canal system.

A theatre critic and opera-lover, Aickman turned his hand to writing 'strange stories' quite late, and produced forty-eight of them published in eight volumes that were eventually recognised as masterpieces of the form. He had the ability to invest the daylight world with all the terrors of the night, and specialised in subverting notions of safety and sunshine into something sinister and unforgiving. His work is best summed up by a wonderful German word, *unheimlich,* meaning 'uncanny', which has the deeper connotation of suggesting the unease caused by being away from home, literally un-home-like.

In 'Ringing the Changes', Gerald and his new wife head off to the coast on their honeymoon, and this sense of unease is present from the outset. The groom is twenty-four years older than his bride, the inn they have chosen is inhospitable, a night walk through the coastal town provides no glimpse of the sea and all the time, church bells peal endlessly. When Gerald asks the hard-drinking landlady why all the town's churches are bell-ringing simultaneously, she tersely replies 'Practice.' Gerald and his wife have stumbled into an annual ritual to wake the dead, on a night when even the sea retreats, but the story's power – like so much of Aickman's work – derives from a deeper sense of humanity. Gerald and his wife are separated first by age and temperament, then by something more physical, and this acts as an intimation of Gerald's own mortality. Thus is a simple ghost story transformed into a classic. Accessible, suspenseful and disturbing, it unites atmosphere and plot together with an occasionally surprising vocabulary ('vaticinations', 'sequacity').

Aickman was nostalgic for a lost world of fens and villages, and it's no surprise that his first collection was produced with Elizabeth Jane Howard, whose marvellously creepy canal tale 'Three Miles Up' has a kinship with Aickman's best work.

Happily, his writing is finally reaching a new audience and is back in print, with paperbacks from Faber & Faber, and some very collectable, elegant hardbacks from Tartarus Press.

100. Richard Marsh

The Beetle was a bizarre hybrid novel of supernatural romantic mystery published in 1897, the same year as *Dracula*, and initially it eclipsed the undead count's sales. Hysterical in tone, it concerned the worshipper of a secret Egyptian cult who possesses mesmeric shapeshifting powers, and his feverish pursuit of a British politician. Filled with swirling smoke, hypnotic commands and weird chemicals, it is told from four separate viewpoints and is really quite unique in the annals of Victorian literature.

But Richard Marsh didn't exist. In an act of prestidigitation worthy of the Beetle himself, he was one of the many aliases of Richard Bernard Heldmann, a high-living swindler who bilked innocent victims all over the country. When Heldmann was sent to jail for eighteen months, he killed his real name and reinvented himself as Marsh, then embarked upon a writing career.

Marsh managed seventy-six novels and collections of short stories, some of them very hurried and poorly written, but there was often an energetic fervour to his prose that has made his editions highly sought after. What's particularly interesting is how many times he wrote about characters with split personalities or false identities who end up in court. *The Mask* features a lunatic female cross-dresser, and there's even a volume called *A Master of Deception.*

Another recurring theme in the novels is a fall from grace or a sudden massive reversal of fortunes. The author managed three novels a year, published through sixteen different houses, and was immensely popular, but *The Beetle* was his best book. Even in this, Marsh couldn't resist subterfuge, for the vampiric insect is actually an old man in a woman's body who can turn into a giant beetle 'with gluey feet'. The creature alters everyone it comes into contact with, smashing up the social order. In fact, almost everyone in the novel seems to shapeshift in some way, the most extreme being a smart young heroine who cuts her hair short and dresses as a tramp.

There's an apocryphal story that Bram Stoker made a bet to see who could write the best supernatural novel that year. Why didn't *The Beetle* survive as well as *Dracula*? It seems much more of a Victorian zeitgeist novel now, and is saturated with that decade's concerns, values and fears. Seventy-five of Marsh's books are out of print, but there's a very nice cheap Pocket Penguin Classic edition of *The Beetle* currently available.

Afterword by Polly Hope
Here, Away From It All

I wrote this story to tell everyone about life on a Greek island in the 1960s, an exotic and little known destination then. The blue skies, the cool wine, the sweet locals, the clever ex pats, the simple and perfect life. Or so we all believed. Then it suddenly wasn't like that any longer and *Here* is exactly what happened. Well maybe I did paint the colours somewhat brighter to enhance the story, but in essence it is all true, and thankfully most of us did survive.

The book was written using a pseudonym, Maryann Forrest, as I didn't want to be thrown out of the country and have my house confiscated, a very likely occurrence then as throwing out foreigners under the Greek Colonels was pretty usual.

Re-reading the book recently for the new edition I can't believe what a nasty time we lived through, yet we stayed on and amazingly I still love Greeks. I daresay we were young, strong, and full of energy, and anyhow couldn't afford to go anywhere else.

Writing wasn't and still isn't my day job. I am a visual artist but bringing up a family on a Greek island it was easier to post a manuscript than send a lorry load of paintings off to market. The family had to be fed and my books did this.

The reception of *Here* was good, lovely reviews and sales which led to further editions, though thankfully my islanders never found out about it. Now I think is the time perhaps that it should appear in Greece.

I subsequently wrote and published two more novels, *Us Lot* and *The Immaculate Misconception*, both somewhat horrific, one set in Wales and the other in Paris, and at the moment am working on a long and complicated novel about The Greek War of Independence in the early 19th century. Not so much horror but plenty of action. Hopefully it will get finished during the next year.